THE BOOK OF ARS
Compiled b

CONTENTS

INTRODUCTION: A brief history of "The Quote".
PART 1: EARLY GUNNERS
PART 2: 1945 to 1986
PART 3: 1986 to 1996
PART 4: THE WENGER YEARS, 1996 ONWARDS

First published in September 2016.
Copyright (c) Fred Atkins

INTRODUCTION:
A brief history of "The Quote".

"The media are enjoying it, the majority of the media are enjoying it. They're enjoying us getting all this stick because normally nothing comes out of Highbury."

The above quote, taken from a speech George Graham gave to the Arsenal squad during the 1990/91 title-winning season, is almost as accurate now, 25 years later, as it was then.

Normally nothing came out of Highbury during the Graham years and even in the twitter era nothing much comes out of The Emirates. That says something for the efficiency of the club's media department and its efforts to maintain the uneasy truce between two permanently suspicious interest groups.

Managers and players believe that journalists and editors are often cynical, manipulative and morally vacuous bastards. Journalists and editors often believe that managers and players are equally cynical, manipulative and morally vacuous bastards.

The result is the modern press conference, a deathly pointless ritual in which footballers say nothing at all, because when they do, journalists make them look like arseholes.

A classic example came when Jack Wilshere gave an honest answer to the question of whether or not Manchester United's Kosovo-born Belgian Adnan Januzaj should be eligible to play for England.

"The only people who should play for England are English people. If you've lived in England for five years, for me, it doesn't make you English. You shouldn't play. It doesn't mean you can play for that country. If I went to Spain and lived there for five years, I'm not going to play for Spain. For me an English player should play for England really."

The idea of the England team picking English players wasn't hugely controversial, but even the supposedly reputable Guardian conjured the headline: "Jack Wilshere enters the Januzaj debate: Keep England for the English." The assertion that Wilshere had "entered the debate" as opposed to "politely answered a question" was dubious, but it was far less damaging than the subtle inference of racism, with the headline echoing an EDL refrain.

This is just one example of what even the more credible news outlets can do to a player and that's before we take into account entities like the Daily Star and Piers Morgan, both of whom swallowed this quote, which supposedly came from Cesc Fabregas.

"If I ever wear a Chelsea shirt you have permission to kill me."

Fabregas was alleged to have said this on Twitter in February 2010, a quote that was retrospectively used to make him look hypocritical, fickle and shallow. It also conveniently overlooked the fact he didn't join Twitter until seven months after the supposedly incriminating tweet.

The role of the quote and its twin brother the misquote hasn't really changed since Herbert Chapman managed Arsenal. Now that almost every interview is recorded outright fabrication is rare, but for as long as reporters have been sticking notepads in front of managers, the potential for words to be taken out of context, twisted and used as a weapon of disinformation has remained constant.

When Chapman was quoted saying, "I don't mind what you write about Arsenal as long as you mention them," over 80 years ago, it could have been taken as evidence of an astute media operator.

But according to one of his eventual successors, Tom Whittaker, Chapman never actually said it - or perhaps more accurately, he might have said it but he certainly wouldn't have meant it.

Chapman demanded accuracy and would berate any journalist he felt had "overstepped the bounds of truth".

Like another of his successors Arsene Wenger, Chapman was aware of the cynicism of the press and realised that the only viable strategy for coping with it was to use this cynicism to his advantage whenever possible.

When that didn't work, such as after a spat with the Daily Mail in the 1930s, Chapman could reflect that he preferred being misquoted to being ignored, but it was with the air of resignation of a man who knew he could only win so many battles.

Writing in the early fifties, Whittaker himself felt the British press showed "dignity and fairness" compared to their South American counterparts when he arrived on a tour of Brazil that offered a nightmarish vision of the future of football journalism.

The gentleman Whittaker read that he was supposed to have claimed: "English Football is the best in the world; Arsenal will win every match" and "Brazilian football is third-rate." By the time he'd called a press conference to protest against this deliberate propaganda the damage was irreversible.

In the matches themselves Brazilian radio reporters were so desperate for quotes that they would actually run onto the field of play after a goal and try to get the scorer to say a few words, something even Sky haven't attempted (yet).

*

The manipulation works both ways however. Managerial press conferences have evolved into sinister, choreographed affairs with "the quote" often a calculated act of bad sportsmanship deliberately designed to unsettle a rival or influence a referee. Apologists refer to this as "Mind Games."

In the build-up to the game that ended Arsenal's 49-game unbeaten run, "Sir" Alex Ferguson referred to the previous season's 0-0 draw at Old Trafford in the following terms:

"They got away with murder. What the Arsenal players did was the worst I have witnessed in sport."

This was, demonstrably, bollocks, but coincidentally or not, United were allowed to get away with a game plan of cynicism unrivalled since Brazil's World Cup quarter-final win over Colombia nearly a decade later, while the United fans sang, "Same Old Arsenal, Always Cheating."

Ferguson is far from the only manager to have stooped to this tactic, but Wenger (whose reaction to the defeat was inevitably portrayed as churlish and unsportsmanlike) tends to avoid it.

He can sound bitter and resentful in "pressers", particularly after defeats, but as a rule he manages to be consistently entertaining and quotable, even though English is not his native language. He regularly produces brilliant, if somewhat surreal analogies and isn't always rewarded for his candour.

At the start of the 2002-03 season Wenger was asked if his team could go the entire season undefeated.

"It's not impossible as AC Milan once did it but I can't see why it's so shocking to say it. Do you think Manchester United, Liverpool or Chelsea don't dream that as well? They're exactly the same. They just don't say it because they're scared to look ridiculous, but nobody is ridiculous in this job as we know anything can happen."

This was an ambitious statement, but it was tempered with caution that was deliberately ignored by journalists and editors who were intent on making Wenger look like an arsehole - which is precisely how a sizable percentage of their readers want him to look.

A sample headline was "Comical Wenger Says We Can Go The Whole Season Unbeaten" and the lie flew several thousand times round the world before the truth had even started to get its pants on.

The role of "the quote" in football has changed out of all recognition since Graham's era, when it was still common to read match reports without any reported speech. Now the "style books" used by most newspapers and agencies compels the writer to use a quote by the third paragraph, regardless of its banality.

Wenger's least interesting quotes come after an Arsenal victory, when he can be relied on to praise the team's "character" and spirit". When things do go wrong his job is to work with the club's media department to protect Arsenal's reputation. As a general rule they do so almost as effectively as Graham's back four once protected David Seaman, but even that backline conceded occasionally. And not even the most effective media department can shut down everything. Take this quote from William Gallas in 2008, in an interview with the Associated Press:

"When, as captain, some players come up to you and talk to you about a player complaining about him and then during the match you speak to this player and the player in question insults us, there comes a time where we can no longer comprehend how this can happen. I am trying to defend myself a bit without giving names. Otherwise I'm taking it all (the blame). It's very frustrating. I'm 31, the player is six years younger than me."

The quote was shocking for a number of reasons.

It was an unprecedented attack by an Arsenal captain on his team mates. It shattered the myth of a united dressing room and left fans wondering if Arsenal's players knew they were supposed to be battling the opposition or each other. It rendered Gallas's position untenable and called into question Wenger's judgement in handing him the role in the first place.

Yet what was most surprising was that the story emerged at all, even though the Arsenal side that season contained personalities like Gallas, Adebayor, van Persie and Nasri, all of whom were capable of starting arguments in the proverbial empty room.

Quotes with that power usually only emerge after a player has left the club. Gallas, however, was trying to sell a book and even the worst autobiography, tossed out into a ghost's dictaphone over the course of a few hours, offers something the press conference almost never can, a genuinely reflective insight into the player's mindset, away from the defensiveness and hostility of a post-match inquisition.

This is why autobiographies are so useful. In some cases, particularly for books that haven't been serialised, they have only been read by a few thousand people and the material seems almost fresh even when it's several years old.

While researching: "Arsenal: The French Connection," I read dozens of player autobiographies, including Ashley Cole's "My Defence," which I acquired for 3p via Amazon.

Cole's book was mercilessly pilloried when it was released in 2006 and his famous quote about nearly crashing his car when he was "only" offered £55,000 per week has been endlessly recycled ever since, yet the full text itself offered several insights that have never really appeared anywhere else, chiefly the fact that his departure for Chelsea could easily have been avoided.

When it was released, Theo Walcott's "Growing Up Fast" was dismissed on the grounds that Walcott was still barely out of his teens when he or his ghost wrote it, but it is an underrated piece of work which contains a couple of beautifully subtle character assassinations of Robin van Persie and Samir Nasri.

In the course of over 125 years there are plenty of similar gems to be found in amongst the sea of platitudes about "never giving up" and "showing our fighting spirit". Some are jaw-droppingly brilliant, others hilarious, many are contradictory and just occasionally, like Alex James' words on his death bed, simply heartbreaking.

Five decades before Walcott was born, Cliff Bastin was showing a similarly dry sense of humour while talking about Alex James and Herbert Chapman was offering the press the kind of quotes one can easily imagine Arsene Wenger saying.

If you had to pick one single quote to sum up the Arsenal it would easy to find the right words, but less easy to find their author.

"Remember who you are, what you are and who you represent."

This is attributed to the late, great David Rocastle on a banner at the Emirates, but Rocky was actually quoting George Graham and before him Don Howe.

The misquote has been with us nearly as long as the quote. Sadly it isn't true that Andy Linighan drives round Hertfordshire with a van that says "Average Footballer, Excellent Plumber" on the side. But does it matter? To paraphrase James Stewart: "This is the Arsenal, Sir. When the legend becomes fact, print the legend.

Fred Atkins, September 2016.

PART ONE
EARLY GUNNERS 1886 to 1945

"Excitement is a mild description for the scenes in Woolwich and Plumstead on the return of the football champions on Saturday night. A host of admirers met them at Dockyard Station and drove them in open carriages, shouting and singing. There were celebrations everywhere all evening and, we fear, a good deal of drinking was mixed with the rejoicing and exultation."
After winning the London Senior Cup in 1891.

SIR HENRY NORRIS
"Photographs and written accounts suggest that Norris was a terrifying man, bearing an uncanny resemblance to Dr Crippen, notorious wife-murderer of the day."
John Spurling, in "Rebels With A Cause."

"Mr Norris has decided that financial gain is more important than protecting our local club. He is making a mistake. You cannot 'franchise' a football club – Woolwich Arsenal must stay near Woolwich. Would Norris advocate moving Liverpool to Manchester? People like him have no place in association football."
A letter to the Kentish Gazette in 1913, quoted in "Rebels With A Cause".

"On the morning of Sat 6 September 1913 with Arsenal due to play their first fixture ever at Highbury, chaos still reigned: the offices and changing rooms weren't connected to the plumbing; the pay boxes at the entrances weren't working; the grandstand's seats still hadn't been fitted; the grandstand had no roof; and workmen and delivery-men were still at work. With a grace and resignation that I don't think he would have displayed later in his life, Henry Norris gave up worrying about it all. Instead he took Alfred Kearney and Humphrey's senior employee on site out to lunch at an Italian restaurant at Finsbury Park. Despite nothing being ready, the fixture went ahead."
The build-up to the first ever match at Highbury, quoted from www.wrightanddavis.co.uk

"We haven't paid any big prices for players. I don't personally believe in big transfer fees."
Norris to "The Candid Critic" of the Islington Gazette, in a very rare interview in 1913. According to Wright and Davis he didn't give another "personal" interview until 1922, although he did respond to calls and questions.

"When I disagreed with him at board meetings, as I soon had to do to justify my own position and stand up for what I knew was best for the club and boys he used to flay me with words until I was reduced to a fuming, helpless silence... Those board meetings took years off my life."
Leslie Knighton in his autobiography.

"It takes at least two to score a goal but that was a fact which I never really got Sir Henry Norris to understand."
Knighton on Norris' tactical awareness.

'Arsenal Football Club is open to receive applications for the position of TEAM MANAGER. He must be experienced and possess the highest qualifications for the post, both as to ability and personal character. Gentlemen whose sole ability to build up a good side depends on the payment of heavy and exorbitant transfer fees need not apply.'
The advert, written by Norris, that led to Herbert Chapman's appointment as Arsenal manager.

"I have never met his equal for logic, invective and ruthlessness against all who opposed him. When I disagreed with him at board meetings and had to stand up for what I knew was best for the club, he used to flay me with words until I was reduced to fuming, helpless silence."
Leslie Knighton.

"The man who always got his own way over everything did not trouble to defend himself, as I knew he could have done, when the blow fell. I wonder why? Was he broken-hearted at this treatment from the game he had loved and on which he had lavished so money, time and care?"
Knighton on Norris' eventual downfall.

DIRTY TRICKS?

"Arsenal had completed one of the most brazen coups in the history of football, overseen by Norris and supported by McKenna, and resentment quickly grew as they enjoyed the trappings of top-flight football while Spurs were sent down a division."
Article on ESPN about the decision to spare Arsenal and relegate Tottenham in 1919.

"Spurs were above Arsenal; and when the first division was extended it was taken for granted by everyone – except Sir Henry Norris – that Spurs would get the place. I have been told they were to do so – but Sir Henry used his influence, which was enormous, speaking to an important person here, reminding a certain financier who was interested that he had once done him a good turn and promised a return of it … to everyone's utter amazement, Arsenal got the place and Spurs were left. Influence and power had once again performed a miracle."
Leslie Knighton, in his autobiography.

"They (Tottenham's supporters) have, since 1919, been involved in one of the most extraordinary attempts in the history of football to re-write history and besmirch the name of another club.
Not only that, but Tottenham's approach has been stunningly successful, with most media regularly re-running the Tottenham storyline, even though it has very little to do with what actually happened in 1919 when Tottenham were relegated, Chelsea given back their place in the first division, and Arsenal promoted."
Tony Attwood, Arsenal History Society, www.blog.woolwicharsenal.co.uk

"Was it bribery and corruption? That might seem a little extreme to allege but then it is exactly what Tottenham have been alleging since 1919, but I don't want to follow their nasty approaches to football history, but instead stick to the facts."
Attwood on how Tottenham managed to get elected into Southern League Division 1.

GEORGE ALLISON

"It's 1-0 to the Arsenal and that's just the way we like it."
In 1939, a line from the film "the Arsenal Stadium Mystery", uttered during the half-time team talk - 45 years before the song "1-0 to the Arsenal" was first sung to the tune of the Pet Shop Boys' "Go West".

"Probably the luckiest football manager of all time."
Eddie Hapgood.

"You are playing Sheffield Wednesday tomorrow and the danger man is Charles Napier. You, Crayston, have the job of marking Napier ... wait a moment let me finish and then give me your views. Don't leave him and don't let him have the ball. And now Crayston, what have you to say?"
"Only this Mr Allinson. Napier plays for Sheffield Wednesday, but we play Blackpool tomorrow."
Jack Crayston spots a flaw in Allinson's team talk.

LESLIE KNIGHTON

"Briefly, my task was to go to Highbury and steadily build up a world-beating team, using all the while the most rigid economy."
His mission.

"Well Knighton, we pay you a great deal of money to advise us and all you can do is sit there as if you were dumb. Can't you talk?"
Sir Henry Norris.

"What the boys require is something in the nature of a courage pill."
The words of a "distinguished West End doctor," who persuaded Knighton to dope his players for a game with West Ham in 1925.

"Getting the boys back to Highbury that afternoon was like trying to drive a flock of angry lions. The pills not only left us raring to go but also developed the most red-hot, soul destroying thirst I've ever known."
Knighton, quite openly admitting to using performance enhancing substances, then apparently legal, before the game with West Ham - which was called off due to fog. The players initially refused to take the pills when the game was rearranged and did refuse to take them before the replay.

HUGH "MIDGIT" MOFFAT

"I've got a little tiny chap waiting for you. Says he's come to play for Arsenal. He's asleep in the dressing-room."
The groundsman, informing Leslie Knighton his new winger, Hugh Moffat, had arrived at Highbury in 1923. Moffat, nicknamed "midget" was just 5"0 tall. Norris had reportedly imposed a minimum height if 5"8 for all new signings.

"As soon as I saw the boy Moffat my heart sank. He was the tiniest adult footballer I had ever set eyes on."
Knighton, who nonetheless still signed Moffat from Workington.

"Nobody under five-feet-eight or eleven stone ... nobody mind!"
The instruction from Norris that Knighton ignored to sign Moffat.

HERBERT CHAPMAN

"Sir Henry arranged for all the costly additions to his team under a sort of hypnotic spell, as I shall always believe, cast over him by Herbert Chapman, one of the most persuasive talkers who ever lived."
Leslie Knighton, barely able to suppress his resentment at Chapman's ability to prise open Norris' wallet.

"No one can amble through a game today, taking rests when the need is felt, and there can be no abuses of training without the penalty being paid. The modern pace would kill the old footballer in a month."

"Can it be believed that the Arsenal, in order simply to produce results, would cultivate a style that did not appeal to the fans?"

"As soon as they got into the 1932 Final the Arsenal players plunged into another life."

"They (Spurs) are rich beyond doubt, but their position was not built up through the transfer system. As a fact, I know that during the years Peter McWilliam was there, they were outstanding as good sellers, and that they received more from the disposal of players than they paid for new ones."

"The time has come when almost every first-class footballer who falls out with his club and demands to be transferred is under suspicion. Suppose, for instance, a prominent member of the Arsenal took up this attitude, I think any club before signing him on would require to know all the circumstances. Why did he want to leave a club where every player was kindly and generously treated, where he was paid as much as the game allows, and where he ought to be satisfied? There might be an adequate reason why he wished to leave, but these are matters which I, at any rate, should want to enquire into. Indeed, one of the first enquiries I make when contemplating the engagement of a man is: "How does he behave; what sort of life does he lead?" Unless the answers are satisfactory, I do not pursue the matter further."

"Today there is only room for the decent fellow in the dressing-room. The social standing of the professional is much higher than it used to be. Most of them are well educated and intelligent, and they resent the intrusion of one who does not conduct himself properly."

"Every one seems to know the business of the football club. It has little or no privacy. Even matters which should be kept secret are broadcast to satisfy a curious world. It is very unfortunate. When I left London in March 1932, in company with Sir Samuel Hill-Wood and Mr. J Edwards, the chairman and vice-chairman of the Arsenal, to negotiate with Sheffield United for the transfer of Dunne, their centre forward, I believed that only the officials of the two clubs had any knowledge of the matter. Judge my astonishment when the ticket-collector at the London station said to me as I was about to get into the train, 'I hope you get him. He's a great player'."

"Whoever heard of Gillespie Road? It is Arsenal around here!"
After persuading the local authorities to change the name of the tube station in 1932.

"A player´s value should be judged on his ability to fit in with the other members of the team. The best player who ever kicked a ball would be small use if he were as one apart. This is the danger of every transfer. No player can be worth his price unless he becomes a team man."

"I will never tolerate slackness. If it enters a team, there can be no success that is worthwhile. That, at any rate, is my view, and frankly I cannot be bothered with any man unless he is prepared to give his whole mind to his job."

"George, this is Mr Wall, my assistant. He will drink whisky and dry ginger. I will drink gin and tonic. We shall be joined by guests. They will drink whatever they like. See that our guests are given double of everything, but Mr Wall's whisky and dry ginger will contain no whisky, and my gin and tonic will contain no gin."
While negotiating the transfer of David Jack from Bolton to Arsenal, in a hotel bar for a then record fee of £10,980.

"I appeal to the authorities to release the brake which they seem to delight in jamming on new ideas, as if wisdom is only to be found in the council chamber. I am impatient and intolerant of much that seems to me to be merely negative, if not actually destructive, legislation."
Arguing for numbers on shirts.

"The keynote of Arsenal football is soundness. It is only when the team are, say, two goals up that they may claim the licence to be spectacular. From this point of view I am beginning to wonder whether adequate credit is given to defence. The truth is you can attack for too long. We try to make it rapid and direct. We do not favour what is called the close-passing game."

"One of the first enquiries I make when contemplating the engagement of a man is: "What sort of a life does he lead?" I will never tolerate slackness."

"I have been told that attending dog racing is better than dancing or the cinema. I emphatically disagree. Dog racing! Gambling can have a very serious influence on footballers. A day on the golf course appeals to them. But they must not have too much golf."

"The man who coined the phrase 'Get rid of it' could have had no idea of the harm it would cause. Not so long ago a young player told me that when he played in the second team the ball seemed as big as a balloon. In the senior side, however, it shrank to the size of a marble."

"It seems I shall never be allowed to forget Walsall. It should be realised that a League match and a cup-tie are entirely different propositions. In one everything is normal; in the other everything is exceptional. Psychological matters enter largely into cup football."
Reflecting on the infamous FA Cup defeat in 1933.

"I borrowed a megaphone and stood up in front, with the intention of informing the people that the match had been officially stopped owing to bad light.
I started: "The referee, a gentleman from Yorkshire…," but I never got any further.
A man shouted: "You come from Yorkshire, and there are no gentlemen there."
The crowd roared, and, still laughing, they left the ground, at once realising that the referee had ordered play to be abandoned; and that was the end of it."

"My remedy for barracking is a simple one. I have never had to contend with the nuisance in any serious form, but if it ever occurred, I would appeal to the fair-mindedness of the crowd, and I believe that there would be sufficient sportsmen among every gathering of spectators to see that it was stopped."

'There is one golden rule: it is never safe to be satisfied. No matter how good the team may be, there should always be an attempt to improve it. It is sometimes suggested that a winning team are got together by luck. This has not been my experience. One has to watch a team like a thermometer."

"I'm always sorry for clubs who have to act hurriedly, for under favourable conditions it is a tricky business. It is not enough that a man should be a good player. The longer I have been on the managerial side, the more I am convinced that all-round intelligence is one of the highest qualifications. Brains today are more important than ever."

"Bad language, gambling and barracking are the chief evils of the game. Professional players, like artists, are highly strung and affected by ill-considered criticism from the crowd."
If only he'd lived to see Twitter.

"In my playing days no attempt was made to organise victory. The day of haphazard football has gone."

"A team can attack for too long. The most opportune time for scoring is immediately after repelling an attack, because opponents are then strung out in the wrong half of the field."
In 1930 - 80 years ahead of his time.

"Spectators are on the whole good judges, though they are liable to be smitten with strange and extraordinary prejudices, especially in regard to individual members of a side."
Chapman on the Highbury crowd.

"The fairness of the Press may never be questioned, and I do not quarrel with the views they express, but I would urge them to try to get beyond the things that are obvious before jumping to conclusions."

"Another incident which I recall points to the incalculable harm which the barracker may do. It was signing-on time some years ago. A youth came into the office, and I put the form before him to sign. To my amazement he covered his face with his hands and burst into tears. "It's no use," he said. "I'm no use to any one in football and I had better get out.

I can't stand it any longer. The crowd are always getting at me. I'm going home and I hope I shall never kick a ball again."

"I have known complaints to be made because a man has 'slanged' a colleague on the field. Alex James once said that old Celtic teams always seemed to be having a row among themselves and that the harder they went for each other the better they played."

"There was an aura of greatness about him. He possessed a cheery self-confidence. His power of inspiration and gift of foresight were his greatest attributes. I think his qualities were worthy of an even better reward. He should have been Prime Minister, and might have been but for the lack of opportunities entailed by his position in the social scale."
Cliff Bastin.

"He was to my mind the only real genius football has ever seen. Picture a middle aged man, genial and smiling, shirt-sleeves rolled up, jacket off. Bubbling over with dynamic personality. A leader of men… I did not like the way Chapman did certain things: he didn't like me either. So we bickered on, neither giving way, both too obstinate to consider the other fellow's point of view."
Alex James, speaking in 1934.

TOM PARKER

"Hop in, I'll get you there."
Parker's words to a panic-stricken Eddie Hapgood as he desperately tried to find a taxi to get to Great Ormond Street Hospital with his son. Parker happened to passing when he saw the Hapgoods in the street. His high-speed drive to the hospital saved Hapgood Junior's life.

EDDIE HAPGOOD

"You really must curb this passion for kicking a ball about, otherwise it might get you into trouble."
Magistrate to Hapgood, aged, 10, after fining him 2s6d for breaking a window and three milk bottles during a street match.

"We are of the British Empire and I do not see any reason why we should give the Nazi salute."
Hapgood to Stanley Rous of the FA, before England's infamous match with Germany in 1938. Hapgood's objection was overruled.

"Although we are professional footballers, we also have human feelings like other people. We read the papers and listen to the wireless and I fancy most of us had the same thoughts where Germany was concerned. That, to put it mildly, and in sporting language, they weren't playing the game."

"I often wish it had been something more lethal I had kicked into his lap that afternoon."
After a clearance from Hapgood hit Mussolini in the stand during an England v Italy match in Rome 1933. Mussolini, who hadn't been paying attention to the game, was incensed.

"It's a bit hard to play like a gentleman when someone closely resembling an enthusiastic member of the mafia is wiping his studs down your legs, or kicking you up in the air from behind."
Hapgood's take on the subsequent rematch in 1934, dubbed "The Battle of Highbury."

"I never played dirty football myself because that type of game never gets you anything but injuries and suspensions."

"Hapgood, EA. Any relation to the Arsenal player? Well you played for a classy team, we'll give you a classy job. Just get down and polish this floor."
Words from a Tottenham supporting corporal to Hapgood after he enlisted in the RAF.

"There was a feeling that once you put on an Arsenal shirt nothing could go wrong, that your team was better than all the others."

"I met only two really dirty players during my whole career. But even then, while I was massaging my bruises, I consoled myself with the fact they couldn't beat me fairly so had to resort to other methods."

ALEX JAMES

"Nobody had greater faith in the qualities of Alex James than Alex James himself, not even Herbert Chapman, and that is saying something."
James' ego is subtly assessed by Cliff Bastin.

"I shall always think that the dead set which was made against him was deliberately manufactured to hurt the club as well as the player. It was one of the meanest things I have ever known, and one of the finest players it has been my pleasure to see almost had his heart broken. That is not an exaggeration."
Chapman on the abuse James received during the 1929-30 season.

"He has always been a wonderful individualist. In Lancashire it was said that Preston North End comprised James and ten others. The statement was also put into the mouth of James that in no circumstances was he ever going to chase an opponent in possession of the ball. James possibly held something like this view when he arrived at Arsenal, and it probably accounted for the idea that he would never be any use to the team. But his mind was big enough to allow him to sink much of his individuality in his play, in order to fit in with the schemes of the team."
Herbert Chapman

"When Alex James was taken to the dressing-room during the Arsenal's opening match with Birmingham in the autumn of 1933, he was in great pain. His ankle had been very badly hurt, and I was anxious that he should go to hospital at once. He declined, however, insisting on being allowed to stay until the game was over.
"When the players came off the field at half-time, he was lying on a table still suffering acutely, but it was evident that his thoughts were still on the match... When he was told that Jack had scored, he raised his head from the table and clapped his hands, telling how deep was his interest in the Arsenal team, even when in so much pain."
Herbert Chapman

"Whenever the conversation turns, amongst sports lovers, to great players of the past, his name is always mentioned. And among followers of Arsenal, memories of a shuffling, puckish little figure, trousers down to its knees and shirt-sleeves flapping hose, will be treasured to the very end."
Cliff Bastin, from his autobiography.

"The wee man said through the dope which was easing his pain, 'Tom, I'm dying ... and I'm frightened.' I consoled Alex and he calmed ... With a smile of thanks he said, 'It's been a fine life, Tom. I've loved every minute of it.'"
James on his deathbed, to Tom Whittaker.

THE 1927 FA CUP FINAL
CARDIFF CITY 1 ARSENAL 0

"The football was mediocre to poor."
The verdict of The Times's anonymous reporter.

"For several weeks the experts had been telling us the final would be a mediocre affair, and their prophecy was amply fulfilled...Cardiff will be declared lucky winners and to a great extent that is true. For 75 of the game's 90 minutes they were the poorer of the two sides."
The Guardian's correspondent.

"I think we were very lucky to win because to be candid Arsenal deserved to do so. This was a rather poor game but we do expect these matches to provide the most skilful display. So much depends on the result that we get anxious and I am sure we all were today. Wales will be delighted ... I should say that Arsenal played a clean, hard, sporting game."
Fred Keenor, Cardiff City's captain.

"It was sheer tragedy. It was also obviously the doom of the Arsenal."
The Guardian, on the mistake by keeper Dan Lewis that led to the only goal, later blamed on the greasiness of his shirt.

"My congratulations to Cardiff City on being the first club in history to take the cup out of England. We did our utmost to prevent them doing so but we did not succeed. Cardiff played an honest, clean game each member of the team obviously striving to do his utmost."
Charlie Buchan

"The crowd was very quiet as it drifted away from the stadium. The ticket system had assured that the majority were London supporters, and the shock to their rather unwarranted optimism was a numbing one."
The Guardian again.

THE 1930 FA CUP FINAL
ARSENAL 2 HUDDERSFIELD 0

"The King, after all, was able to visit Wembley, and never has he received a more spontaneous and enthusiastic greeting from an English crowd."
PJ Moss, on George V's first public appearance for 18 months due to septicaemia.

"The deafening roar from its engines disconcerted both players and spectators. The giant aircraft, at 775 ft in length, was a symbol of a rising Germany, and it dipped its nose in salute to King George V as it passed by."
Arsenal.com on the sinister arrival of the Graf Zeppelin, which flew just a few metres over the ground, while the match was in play.

"Alex was fouled somewhere near the penalty area, and, almost before the ball had stopped rolling, had taken the free-kick. He sent a short pass to Cliff Bastin, moved into position to take a perfect return, and banged the ball into the Huddersfield net for the all-important first goal. Tom Crew told me that James made a silent appeal for permission to take the kick, and he waved him on. It was one of the smartest moves ever made in a big match and it gave us the Cup. I contend that it was fair tactics; for if Alex had waited a few seconds for the whistle, the Huddersfield defence would have been in position, and the advantage of the free-kick would have been lost."
Eddie Hapgood's view of the opening goal.

"Never was a match contested in a more sporting spirit. And never, even going back to the earliest days of football, was the game played in a cleaner manner."
Moss again. At the behest of Herbert Chapman the two teams dined together after the match.

It was glorious and pulsating from start to finish, an entirely different atmosphere from that of of two internationals in which I have participated at Wembley."
Alex James.

"This was not a good final."
The Times' CRC Dixon disagrees.

THE 1932 FA CUP FINAL
NEWCASTLE UNITED 2 ARSENAL 1

'Cup Final goal was not a goal. Film proves it – yet it must stand'.
Daily Herald headline, of the world's first great refereeing controversy.

"The story of this equalising goal, in plain words, is that forty minutes after the start Boyd screwed the ball in when it was just over the goal line. Allen took possession and promptly shot into the net, the referee was well up with the play and without the slightest hesitation signalled for a goal. There was no counter Arsenal demonstration. The London players never make scenes on the field, irrespective of the class of match in which they may be playing."
The Times.

"From my position I could not see whether it had gone out of play or not."
Newcastle manager Andy Cunningham.

"It was a goal. As God is my judge, the man was in play."
Referee WP "Percy" Harper in the Manchester Guardian. Harper subsequently received death threats and letters accusing him of fixing the match.

CLIFF BASTIN

"Clifford Bastin signed professional forms on his seventeenth birthday, and I had no hesitation in putting him almost at once into the Arsenal side, for he was a most exceptional boy. I have never known a youth with the same stability as Bastin. Temperamentally, so far as football is concerned, he is like a block of ice, untouched by excitement."
Herbert Chapman

PART TWO: 1945 TO 1986
TOM WHITTAKER

"Herbert Chapman worked himself to death for the club and if that is my fate, I am happy to accept it."

Speaking in 1947, quoted on the Arsenal Collective website. He died of a heart attack nine years later.

THE 1950 FA CUP FINAL

"Why did we lose Dad? Liverpool's the best team in the world so why did we lose? Why didn't Billy Liddell score? We were robbed weren't we?"

Scouse "comedian" Jimmy Tarbuck, aged 9, to his father as revealed to Ken Jones of the Daily Mirror.

"Two weeks before the Cup final, we played Arsenal at Highbury and we beat them. And a few weeks previous to that we played them at Anfield and also beat them, without any bother, so we fancied our chances at Wembley."

Liverpool's centre-forward Albert Stubbins.

"I can't describe just how I felt when I learned I was out of the Wembley side. It is the sort of thing you only dream, or rather have nightmares about."

Bob Paisley, Liverpool's future manager, on being dropped, despite scoring the winner in the semi-final against Everton.

"When Arsenal and Liverpool qualified for Wembley I was no longer allowed to train with the Liverpool players. I used to train on my own in the afternoon but whenever I bumped into the Liverpool players I told them they were certain to beat us in the final. I fostered their confidence and it gave us an advantage."

Joe Mercer, who was still living and training on Merseyside.

"Arsenal won by superior strategy. They took note of Mercer's ripening years and fading stamina and turned these into positive advantages. Mercer stationed himself well downfield, only slightly in front of Walley Barnes and in close touch with Les Compton. This meant that Mercer could move quickly to Compton's aid if danger threatened down the centre, or to Barnes's aid if Payne showed any signs of becoming troublesome on the wing."

The Guardian's Donny Davies.

"Proper terrible, isn't it? Well fancy that, would you believe it."

An abysmal attempt by the commentator to impersonate a Liverpool fan, after footage of Lewis' second goal went in, which ended up sounding more Brummie than Scouse.

"I allowed no Arsenal supporters into the house apart from Robert Wyatt ... until the mid 1990s."

DJ John Peel, who supported Liverpool from this game onwards, despite clearly being traumatised by the result.

"This is the greatest moment of my life to be holding the cup here at Wembley and while we're very, very pleased to have won it I would like to say how wonderful the Liverpool boys have been in their defeat."
Joe Mercer.

"I thought the biggest honour in football was to captain England, but I was wrong. It was to captain Arsenal today."
Joe Mercer, (this quote is attributed to Mercer about both the 1950 final and the 1952 final, which Arsenal lost.)

BILLY WRIGHT

"I want to bring trophies back to Highbury and get people talking about Arsenal again for the right reasons."
After being named as George Swindin's replacement in 1962.

"This is the most disappointing day of my whole life … It was heartbreaking for me. Maybe I was too nice, but that is the way I am. But I wanted so much to make Arsenal great again, and I did feel that with the young players we were moving along the right lines."
After his resignation in 1966.

"Billy has never given up anything in his life. He has been forced into it."
Wright's wife Joy, one of the Beverley sisters, debunks the idea the resignation was voluntary.

"He had neither the guile nor the authority to make things work and he reacted almost childishly to criticism."
Brian Glanville offers a less charitable view of Wright's tenure, in his book Wright or Wrong?

"The youth policy was just about beginning to bear fruit and now it seems that someone else will reap the benefit."
Seven players from the youth team, Wilson, Rice, Simpson, Storey, Sammels, Radford, Armstrong, would win the double under Bertie Mee.

BERTIE MEE

"Outside of quality, we had other qualities."

"If you want them moved you'll just have to replace them,"
Mee's reply when Frank McLintock asked for pictures of former captain's displaying trophies to be moved out of sight at Highbury.

"I would not normally say this as a family man, but I am going to ask you for the sake of this football club to put your family second for the next month. You have the chance to put your names in the record books for all time."
Mee after winning the FA Cup semi-final replay with Stoke in 1971.

"When he spoke I tended to drift off."
Charlie George.

"He's not a football man, is he Charlie?"
Bill Shankly to George, when both were at Derby.

"A cold, pompous man."
Charlie George again.

DON HOWE
"At the end of the day, the Arsenal fans demand that we put eleven players on the pitch."

PETER STOREY
"It's about the drunken parties that go on for days, the orgies, the birds and the fabulous money."
Storey on his priorities.

"The trick was to get in early as possible, hit them hard, give them a good wallop, make them feel as if they'd been in a car crash or hit a brick wall."

"I usually put them to the keepers' right. Then I thought hang on, this is Banksie. He'll know that. So the other side it goes."
On the FA Cup semi-final penalty that earned Arsenal a replay against Stoke.

"What a responsibility. A last-minute penalty in an FA Cup semi-final and faced by Gordon Banks, the world's number one keeper. But Peter never opts out of anything. He makes things happen where others might prefer to wait for them to happen. He walked up and stuck it away, he was tremendous."
Bertie Mee in the Mirror.

"The bastard's bastard."
Barney Ronay of the Guardian.

"It was as if I had spent ages making love to the most beautiful woman in the world only to be kicked out of bed five minutes before the climax."
On fearing he would be dropped for the 1971 FA Cup Final.

"I got away with things which would get me locked up today, but I never broke anyone's leg and I don't recall doing any serious long-term damage to end anyone's career. There is nothing 'hard' about flying into a tackle at 100mph and breaking someone's leg. That's not commitment, or passion, or whatever they call it today – it's cowardly."
Storey, revealing his moral code to the Mirror's Mike Walters.

CHARLIE GEORGE
"Three-and-a-half years later I had gone from standing there shouting out the players' names to actually playing with those guys."

"I liked a fight and I always stood up for myself. That's how I was brought up. Coming from Holloway you learn from the pram to nut people who pick on you."

"Shave that off. You will not play for Arsenal until you do."
Bertie Mee, on seeing George with a beard.

"He could ping the ball with the outside of his foot like Franz Beckenbauer and it would zip 40 yards, right on target: he made it appear so easy it could have been a tennis ball."
Frank McLintock

"Cruyff was almost as good as myself."

"KING CHARLIE WIPES THE FLOOR WITH AJAX"
Headline after Arsenal's Fairs Cup win in 1970.

"Unfortunately I wasn't involved."
Charlie on the brawl with Lazio, September 1970.

"I told him in no uncertain terms to go and fuck himself."
George to 'Uncle' Don Revie after being substituted on what was his only appearance for England.

"I didn't do it out of meanness. Just for a bit of a laugh."
On why he didn't help Bertie Mee to climb out of hole he'd fallen into during a cross country run on a pre-season tour of Sweden. George reportedly told Mee to "fuck off" instead.

BOB WILSON

"That was a major problem for my dad. My two older brothers were killed during the war. Jock was a Spitfire pilot, shot down and killed before he was 20, and Billy was a rear gunner in a Lancaster, shot down and killed before he was 21. So there were two heroes I could never live up to, and who I never knew."
On having the German Bert Trautmann as his boyhood hero.

THE 1970 FAIRS CUP FINAL

"Come on lads! Van Himst's a cart horse. Their centre half is awful! Get crosses in! We'll beat this lot!"
Remarks allegedly made by Frank McLintock, about Anderlecht play-maker Paul van Himst during a post-match rallying call following the first leg in Brussels, which Arsenal lost 3-1.

"A RAY OF HOPE"
Mirror headline after Ray Kennedy's late goal in Brussels.

"I didn't have time to take aim I just let go and hoped for the best. I could have jumped out of the stadium when I saw it go into the top of the net."
Eddie Kelly, on the goal that made it 1-0 to the Arsenal in the second leg, quoted on arsenalhistory.com

"The second leg we were amazing. The atmosphere at Highbury was like never before or since – relief and joy. It took me 20 minutes to get to the changing rooms afterwards because I was stuck amongst the fans. In fact I remember nearly being strangled by one fan who grabbed a scarf around my neck."
McLintock, after the second leg.

"It was so special because, for me, it was all for those long-suffering supporters, particularly the older ones who had stuck with the Club during some bad times. They had seen the glory many years before and had to wait a long time.
Jon Sammels, talking to Arsenal's official website.

"It meant I wasn't a jinx or a loser anymore. It meant I could look people like Joe Mercer in the eye."
McLintock again.

"The experience we gained tonight will be invaluable for winning our next objective – the Football League."
Bertie Mee.

WHITE HART LANE 1971

"Arsenal have got as much chance of being handed the title by Spurs as I have of being given the Crown Jewels. They are the last people we want winning the Championship."
Alan Mullery.

"Our lives wouldn't be worth living ... I don't think our supporters would ever forgive us if we lost and it will go down in history if we stop Arsenal winning the championship."
Mullery again.

"That was the longest three minutes I have ever known. As Tottenham came back I remember thinking that perhaps it might have been better had my header not gone in."
19-year-old Ray Kennedy, after heading the only goal. Arsenal had to either win, or draw the game 0-0, to win the title.

"What's a bit of pain on a night like this? This is the most fantastic night of my life."
Bob Wilson, who played on despite a gashed ear.

"This is only the start. Our next target is to win the European Cup and I don't think there is a team around that can stop us."
Don Howe.

"Bill Shankly here. Put that man Bertie Mee on the line… A tremendous performance Bertie, magnificent. You may even give us a game at Wembley on Saturday."
Shankly offers Mee his congratulations.

"Arsenal have had a magnificent season and it has been a magnificent fight. We have not lost the title, they have won it. They are true champions."
Leeds United manager Don Revie.

"Perhaps it is Spurs who have really done us in the end because they beat us at Leeds and now comes this final result."
Jack Charlton of Leeds.

THE 1971 FA CUP FINAL

"We've got to Wembley with a team of boys. We've a pool of players that will last for ten years. And we've not just come for the fun - we've come to win the FA Cup."
Bill Shankly.

"I'll crack a few gags, gee the lads up a bit. That's what Shanks likes."
Jimmy Tarbuck, Liverpool's secret weapon, talking to the Daily Mirror on how he planned to help bring about Arsenal's downfall.

"Good old Arsenal? No, it's going to be poor old Arsenal."
Mystic Tarby again.

"A goalie should never move off his post as Wilson did. He may have been distracted by Toshack but his first job is always to stop the direct threat."
Jimmy Hill on ITV, discussing his future BBC colleague's role in the Liverpool goal at the 1971 FA Cup Final.

"I never thought I had even kicked it until I saw the film."
Eddie Kelly on the equaliser.

"I fell down because I didn't have another drop of energy left in me. I wasn't thinking that I ought to do something that people will remember. I was just f***ing knackered. As for that rumour about me having an erection while I was lying there, that's b******s. I never got an erection after scoring a goal."
Charlie George.

"People say why did I lie on the floor after the goal, they said I was tired. But I think I was a lot cleverer than people thought."
Charlie George.

"I can still recall the moment as if it was yesterday, and I can assure you Norman was just exhausted. It was a baking, hot afternoon, and down on the pitch the temperature was up into the 90s, and while Norman's gesture might have looked strange it was merely an expression of relief that he lasted the course. It was like crossing the finish line in a marathon and there was nothing more to Norman's gesture than that. He was just plain knackered because the game spilled over into extra time."
Bob Wilson on referee Norman Burtenshaw's alleged celebration at full-time. Burtenshaw was seen punching the air.

"It was a hot day. The sun was beating down and it drained all my energy. For some reason we were wearing heavy, thick, long sleeved shirts. I may be accused of making excuses for my own bad performance, but I'm convinced that our choice of shirts cost us the trophy - especially as we went into a gruelling extra time."
Emlyn Hughes, not making excuses.

"The Cup was there for the winning. I thought a break would win it - and Arsenal got a break for their equaliser. One goal in extra time is enough to win any game. You don't give away goals like that equaliser. Ray Clemence was coming for the ball thinking Tommy Smith was leaving it and Tommy deflected it past him. It hit Graham on the leg and bounced in."
Shankly.

"My lasting memory is being down on my knees in one of the dressing room toilets after the game, being violently sick. I don't know why I was so ill. My pre-match build-up was the same as usual. Almost certainly it was down to my bitter disappointment."
Tommy Smith.

"They're fair judges, I can't disagree can I? No, don't put that down. I was joking."
George Graham on learning he'd been voted man-of-the-match.

"I want that gentleman in the maroon suit removed from this dressing room. I'm sorry, you were asking how do I feel? That is a factual thing, talking to you that's all I can say. It's a factual thing."
An apparently distracted and incoherent Bertie Mee to Hunter Davies, then a Sunday Times reporter.

"Getting Mr Shankly to give Arsenal credit or even let their name soil his lips was impossible. Had he heard that Mr Mee thought the chances had been 6-2 in Arsenal's favour? 'I'm not interested in talking about Mr Mee. And I'm not interested in talking to you.'"
The final paragraph of Hunter Davies' report.

"Of course I didn't expect Liverpool to play any better. Where are they in the league, eh?"
Charlie George.

"Only chairman Mao in China could turn out a show of strength equal to this - and his would be forced."
Shankly after Liverpool were greeted by 100,000 fans on their return to Merseyside, as they had been in 1950.

"You have been fantastic. I never thought you would be able to out-shout the Kop, but today you did."
Frank McLintock at Islington Town Hall, after an estimated crowd of 250,000 saw the parade from Highbury.

"It was a victory for character. We were a hell of a side to beat."
Frank McLintock.

"My first football memory was Charlie George's goal to win the Double in 1971. After that game I decided to become an Arsenal fan"
Paul Davis.

"Don't ask me to lie on the floor, I'll never be able to get back up!"
George to photographers during a photoshoot at the Emirates in 2014, ahead of Arsenal's fifth round FA Cup tie with Liverpool - which they also won 2-1.

THE 1972 FA CUP FINAL
LEEDS UNITED 1 ARSENAL 0

"Oh the sustained unpleasantness of it all!"
The Sunday Times' Brian Glanville, lamenting a brutal final.

"Lorimer laid it on a bit thick. I only mistimed my tackle... when I went up for my medal the Duke of Edinburgh said he would appear for me at a personal hearing!"
Bob McNab on the tackle that got him booked after 48 seconds, the earliest ever caution in an FA Cup Final.

"Clarke! 1-0."
David Coleman's classically simple commentary on the game's only goal.

"Over the years I've lost count of how many people have asked me about the goal and introduced me to their children who weren't even born in 1972. It means so much to so many Leeds United supporters, and it's a very special memory in my football career. Even now when we play Arsenal at Elland Road, supporters sing 'Who put the ball in the Arsenal net, Allan Allan, Who put the ball in the Arsenal net, Allan, Allan Clarke' and that's a wonderful feeling."
Allan Clarke on mightyleeds.co.uk

"Arsenal could have tried for another hundred years and still would not have had a serious chance of beating Leeds in this centenary FA Cup final at Wembley. Not on the form, the mood and the manpower seen in this match, which never looked like keeping any pre-match promise of developing into one of the truly memorable occasions. But the vast majority of what was best about it came from and belonged to Leeds."
Frank McGhee of the Sunday Mirror.

"Hundredth birthdays are usually marked by a letter of congratulation from the Queen. At half time on Saturday a message of sympathy would have been more appropriate, the participants apparently having decided to mark the occasion as well as each other, by committing one foul for each year. The statisticians were kept busy. Midway through the match, someone cried 'Full house!' meaning that every outfield player had been penalised at least once. The refereeing of David Smith has been described as impeccable in one quarter while another claimed yesterday that he set an early note of 'high authority', no doubt remembering that his job with the Midland Electricity Board involved the scaling of poles."
David Lacey in the Guardian

"Who was badly hurt other than Mick Jones, who fell on his own elbow? Our teams respect each other. And if the game seemed hard, well that was down to finding out the truth of each other's qualities. Where's the satisfaction in playing well just because you've been allowed to?"
Peter Storey.

THE 1978 FA CUP FINAL
IPSWICH TOWN 1 ARSENAL 0

"In the summer after the cup final my wife was in a shoe shop in Ipswich and I was looking in the window and this little lady was tugging at my sleeve. She said 'excuse me. Are you Roger Osborne?' and I said ' yes' and she said 'you made my husband the happiest man the world. He had been a season-ticket holder for many years and he died recently, but he died a happy man."

Roger Osborne, scorer of the only goal, talking to the Ipswich Star in 2008. Osborne collapsed after scoring and had to be revived with smelling salts.

THE 1979 FA CUP FINAL
ARSENAL 3 MANCHETER UNITED 2

"Both Alan and I went for David Price's cross and it is impossible to say who got the final touch. But who cares?"

Brian Talbot on whether he or Alan Sunderland had scored the first goal.

"You grow up reading the comics, and this is the dream, scoring the winning goal in the last minute of an FA Cup final. We were 2-0 up at half-time and then everything was stood on its head by two quick goals by Manchester United. We didn't give goals away in those days. A million things went through my head and I think I went on autopilot. When I scored, it was a total release of pent-up emotion."

Alan Sunderland.

"The worst and the best four minutes of my life."

Pat Jennings.

"I was dreading extra time, I was really tired."

Liam Brady.

"It shouldn't happen to a dog, but Manchester United didn't have a bit of luck all day."

Bobby Charlton.

"This final may not be remembered for flowing football but it will live on in everyone's memory for its explosive finish."

Terry Neill.

"People talk about how the match was a classic. I think the match was fairly average, it was the ending that was amazing. ... When it went to 2-2 I had this horrible feeling in my stomach and the Arsenal team were on the floor, but 60 seconds later we were euphoric. There was no in-between, we went from the most unbelievable low to the most incredible high in the space of a minute."

Frank Stapleton.

"Unbelievable. There is no feeling like it. As to what came out of mouth, it is unprintable. Every foul word imaginable, in an explosion of relief."

Alan Sunderland.

"The day seems to belong in a different lifetime when I watch the highlights now, either that or it's someone else scoring!"
Sunderland, speaking in 2007.

PAT JENNINGS

"Tottenham were leaving to go on tour to Sweden. I went down to say cheerio to the boys and let my team mates know that when they came the next week I wouldn't be there. And the chairman, the directors, when I walked past them in the car park totally blanked me... there was only one place I was going after that and that was over the road."
On leaving Spurs after 14 years' service.

"The Arsenal fans thought it was Christmas. It was the craziest thing Tottenham ever did, just a ridiculous decision to allow him to go to the old enemy."
Bob Wilson.

"I'm Tottenham through and through, I'd never have dreamt about joining Arsenal."

"I think I knew from day one I couldn't teach Pat Jennings anything. He was a far greater goalkeeper than myself."
Bob Wilson.

LIAM BRADY

"My mother always talked a lot and she told Arsenal's chief scout that I'd be OK as long as I was given lots of chips, so the chief scout said: 'We'll call him Chippy'. In that one second, I was given a nickname which lasted throughout my eight years at Arsenal. Strange. I was never called that in Ireland, or anywhere else."
To Hunter Davies in an interview for the Independent in 1992

"The chief scout kept ringing me, wanting me to come back, but he handled it well, never bullying me. After three weeks, I began to miss Arsenal, so I decided to go back. I was never homesick again. Ever."
On his decision to belatedly return to Arsenal after failing to return from a Christmas break in Dublin. Brady was only 15 at the time.

"Oh and Brady won it beautifully ... look at that! Look at that!"
John Motson's commentary on Brady's stunning volley in the 5-0 win at White Hart Lane in 1978.

"The ball came out to Peter Taylor. I took it off him, saw the empty space in the far corner and curved it."
Brady, making the above goal sound almost easy.

(Frank Skinner) "That must have spoilt Christmas for the Tottenham fans."
"They don't celebrate Christmas do they?"
Line delivered slightly awkwardly by Brady during a "Phoenix From The Flames" recreation of the goal on the BBC's Fantasy Football show, with Skinner and the (Jewish) comedian David Baddiel.

"Brady was a midfield player, a passer, and Arsenal haven't really had one since he left. It might surprise those who have a rudimentary grasp of the rules of the game to learn that a First Division football team can try to play football without a player who can pass the ball, but it no longer surprises the rest of us."
Nick Hornby in Fever Pitch.

"I wanted to be up front with the club and the fans. I'd seen how well Kevin Keegan had done in Germany, so I fancied going there. I'll admit the money was a big attraction, but it wasn't the number one reason. I just wanted to live and play football abroad."
After deciding to leave for Juventus, who offered him five times what he was earning at Highbury.

"After one match, I said to Marco Tardelli, let's go for a beer. I was ordering my third glass, and he said he'd have to go, he'd finished. I was amazed. I was just getting warmed up. I soon learnt that in Italy, they don't go out drinking for the evening, not the way we do."

"They made it out to be some kind of wonderful professional gesture on my part not to miss it purposely because I had been told that I wouldn't be wanted and more. A lot of Italian people seemed to think I would have been within my rights to kick it wide, but that didn't go through my mind."
After scoring the penalty that won Juventus the Serie A title.

"I was told when I joined about 'Celtic's paranoia'. Now I know it's true. We are hard done by. Religiously and politically, there are people against us. I meet people who hate me, just because I'm the manager of Celtic. I've had to grow mentally stronger."
During a troubled spell in charge of Celtic that coincided with an era of Rangers domination.

"If my Granny had balls she'd be my grandad."
After a chastening 2-2 draw as Brighton manager against non-league Canvey Island in 1995.

"The way Arsene plays football is the same way I could play football, so we're very compatible in that sense."
Back with Arsenal and in charge of the youth system, a happier Brady talks about working with a kindred spirit.

FRANK STAPLETON

"I've been there a couple of times, I think if I was to walk out on the pitch I wouldn't. When I first went back after leaving, I got stick and it continued thereafter, but that's part and parcel for supporters. They wouldn't boo you if they didn't rate you, so I kind of look on that as a kind of compliment."

"I never wanted to leave Arsenal. I felt they forced me. Liam never wanted to leave either. We both felt we were taken for granted. Players who had never kicked a ball for the club were coming in and we weren't in their bracket when it came to wages."

ALAN SUNDERLAND

" I would have loved to have been there with my dad. We were at home in Yorkshire watching the match. My mum was German. She and dad had met in Dortmund when he was in the army. Mum had gone out shopping, even though I think she wanted to watch it. She couldn't be there. There was too much of a conflict of interest."
On the 1966 World Cup final.

"I was drinking myself to death. I needed to get away."
After spending four years as a publican in Ipswich following his retirement.

DAVID O'LEARY

"When I am asked why I stayed so long the answer is simple, I never wanted to be anywhere else. I could have earned a lot more by moving, but that wouldn't compensate for all the good years with a great club."

LEE CHAPMAN

"Crap."
Kenny Sansom's verdict on Terry Neill's new striker in 1982.

CLIVE ALLEN

"Clive. Oh Clive. Lovely lad. Smashing lad. I went for him because we knew Frank [Stapleton] was going. We went to QPR to see their chairman. A car salesman. Me and Dennis Hill-Wood. Their chairman was telling us he could do the deal on credit and everything. In the end Dennis looked up and said "No. We will pay cash."
Terry Neill, in an interview with Les Crang of the 7amkickoff blog

"Well, it was a good deal. Sammy Nelson's knee was going. He was off to Brighton soon after. Also, Paul Barron was part of the deal. Paul was a fantastic keeper, and Palace needed a goalie, Paul was a tremendous keeper, but Pat [Jennings] just kept playing. It was a good deal all round."
A not entirely convincing response to the same interview by Neill when he was asked why he sold Allen two months later.

KENNY SANSOM

"We shouldn't have been that happy. We should have cared more. With hindsight the speed of how quickly we'd all managed to get over this FA cup disappointment was a travesty. We were all playing well as individuals. But as for knitting together and going out there as a unit who could deliver enough to be winners, it just wasn't happening. We were way off the mark and so the silverware eluded us."
Sansom on the response to an FA Cup defeat to Everton in 1981.

"Lots of fans wanted to know why I was wearing a dodgy Arsenal cap, and I don't know why. Someone must have plonked it on my head and I had far too many wonderful thoughts racing through my mind to think about taking it off. All I wanted to do was get my hands on that beautiful Littlewoods Cup."
On his choice of headgear when lifting Arsenal's first trophy for eight years, the 1987 League Cup.

"Sign me or sell me."
Sun headline after Arsenal bought Nigel Winterburn as a replacement left-back.

"It was I who was my own worst enemy, not George and Arsenal... the tabloid headline had wound George up; perhaps that was what I wanted. I'm not sure. All I know is that I wasn't happy and something had to change. I had reacted to a situation that, in my opinion, would never have arisen had I been properly informed George's reasoning. But that again was the arrogance of the booze and of always having to blame someone else."

"I only bloody scored! But it was disallowed. 'Offside,' ruled the referee. 'Offside my backside!' I yelled back. But the referee wasn't listening. Do you realise that, had my goal stood, Arsenal wouldn't have won the League that season?"
Sansom on being denied an equaliser for Newcastle in a game Arsenal won 1-0 during the title run in in 1988/89. Unknown to the players and many fans the Hillsborough tragedy was unfolding at exactly the same time.

"I drank nine bottles of wine a day."

"A couple of months ago, I was found sleeping in a church yard. I was there for about three or four days in different places. I used to have drink in the daytime and then crash out. I was only drinking three bottles of wine a day. I was drinking slowly because I didn't have a lot of money on me. I'm in detox now. They [The PFA] have helped immensely."
To Radio 5 in 2013 after admitting he'd been sleeping rough.

"I've got no money, I rely on my pension and the jobs that come in. I've not got a contract for jobs and I'm looking forward to going back and working on a regular basis.
I lost my home gambling and drinking. I couldn't pay the mortgage. I was spending the money and it was actually under my wife's name and it just got taken away.
I thought I lost everything, so I felt I might as well have a drink. That's what makes me forget about it all. It was a coward's way out, and I did it."

STEVE WILLIAMS

"Don Howe made me a substitute for the Spurs game and he sent me on for about two minutes to go. What was the point of that, I got on, made one run down the wing, put over one cross and the whistle went."
On his debut after joining from Southampton in 1984.

STEWART ROBSON

"I told Don Howe and George Graham that the boy couldn't play. And he was supposed to be England's next big thing. What a joke."
Steve Williams.

"There is only one person to blame and that's the manager. The person who runs Arsenal is Arsene Wenger. The board don't dictate to him, he dictates to them. So it's his policy that they don't spend big money and big wages."
Robson on the "crisis" in the summer of 2012.

"People like Olivier Giroud, Philippe Senderos, Denilson, Marouane Chamakh, Armand Traore, Sebastien Squillaci, Nicklas Bendtner, Carlos Vela, Emmanuel Eboue, Park Chu-Young, Lukasz Fabianski, Gervinho and Andre Santos. These are the sort of players who Arsene Wenger said were going to be world class players class players and they haven't done it."
Robson in 2013, on players not living up to expectations.

"This is a guy who worked for this club up to a few weeks ago, doing the pre-match stuff on the opposition, who then went to a newspaper, without naming anybody who had given him the so-called facts about him (Arsene Wenger) being a dictator. Today, he's been on every half hour on Radio Five Live, and this is a guy who obviously is a bitter guy because he's no longer got a role or any employment here."
Bob Wilson.

CHARLIE NICHOLAS
"I hired the ostrich outfit for three years running. I loved it. It had the false legs down the side, you know? A few of the lads started implying that there was something sexual about it."
On the annual fancy dress party.

"When I first started getting called Champagne Charlie, I couldn't afford champagne! I was on the shandy, if I was lucky."

"I didn't score as many as I hoped, but it was nice that I always seemed to score against Tottenham."

"Everyone knew the script. Whenever Ian Rush scored for Liverpool they never lost. And as he'd played more than 300 games and scored 200 times, a replay at the very least had been secured. Especially with that mullet-headed ponce Charlie Nicholas (who'd foolishly chosen London's nightclubs ahead of Anfield four years earlier) leading their attack."
Brian Reade, from the book "44 years with the same bird," on the 1987 League Cup Final.

DAVID DEIN
"I think he's crazy. To all intents and purposes it's dead money."
Chairman Peter Hill-Wood on Dein's decision to buy a 16 percent stake in Arsenal in 1983.

"I felt his attitude suggested he was doing me a favour, like I was a 17-year-old trainee."
Ashley Cole on Dein's negotiating technique.

"I love him for his total Arsenalness. He's one of those people who'll always come up to you, shake your hand, ask how things are going and then stiff you in the nicest possible way. He offered us Matthew Upson on loan in 2001 for a salary of £10,000 a week - we took him for two months, then later found out his Arsenal salary was half that. And every time we met in 2000 he'd offer me Christopher Wreh - that was his favourite 'favour'. I've learnt a lot."
Simon Jordan, then chairman of Crytsal Palace, in a column for the Observer.

"Roman Abramovich has parked his Russian tanks on our lawn and is firing £50 notes at us."
After rejecting a bid for Henry and Vieira.

"David Dein is the kind of person who will do you favours that you just don't want. Every time I see David Dein at a social event he has got a player for me who has probably got one leg and he will do me a favour by letting me have him for twice the price."
Simon Jordan again.

PART THREE
1986 TO 1996

GEORGE GRAHAM

"In football, yeah, sometimes you get these multi-talented individuals where that's all they want to do: when the team's got the ball, I'll play but, when we haven't got the ball, I'll go and have a rest."

"I didn't run around at 100mph, which is why I was called stroller."

"To be honest I'd have preferred to have played for a successful Manchester United than a successful Arsenal. They are a bit more fanatical up there and I would have found life more exciting."
Revealing quote in the Evening Standard in the build-up to the 1979 final.

"The linesman is your best friend."
Graham's mantra for the back four.

"It's fine that people hate us. It's part of our history."

"Just run in behind them. They're knackered."
Graham to Perry Groves before his pivotal substitute's role in the 1987 League Cup Final with Liverpool.

"A group of players who liked to spend 90 minutes buzzing angrily round the referee like red and white wasps."
Nick Hornby on Graham's Arsenal teams.

"David O'Leary was getting kicked all over the place by Norman Whiteside, David Rocastle was provoked so much that he got sent off and there was a big row coming off the pitch. Alex Ferguson and his then assistant Archie Knox were right in our faces and I thought: 'Jesus Christ! That'll be the first and last time they intimidate us. We're not going to be bullied any more.'"
After losing to United at Old Trafford in 1987.

"I drove home thinking 'you tight Scots bastard' it's not your money."
Groves, after having a request for a pay rise turned down by Graham.

"The media are enjoying it, the majority of the media are enjoying it. They're enjoying us getting all this stick because normally nothing comes out of Highbury. Again lads, there's one way to handle it. Just keep winning matches. They're looking at us and the stick we've had in the last couple of weeks. It seems fashionable just now to jump on the bandwagon and get at the Arsenal."

"He was paying, so I made sure I caned him on that."
Perry Groves, on the meal that celebrated the 1990-91 title.

"You're Arsenal players and you're having your picture taken with a **** like that! It's just not on."
Graham to Ian Wright and Michael Thomas, after the duo were pictured with the "actress" who nearly ended David Mellor's political career.

Under Graham's regime – it's like saying you'd live in Iraq under Saddam. It was the same regime. He was disgusting, sick. I came to training one day and Graham called another player over, saying "come to my office", but then they just stood in the open so that we could hear everything. Graham said: "I've sold you to Leeds". The player said "I don't want to leave" but Graham responded "Just pack your stuff and go". Do you get it? What a pig."
Anders Limpar, on a Swedish chat show (quoted on the Gingers 4 Limpar website. The player - it's reasonable to deduce, must have been David Rocastle.)

"In fact, I actually had a T-shirt made up which said: "I AM TRYING TO BUY A MIDFIELD PLAYER!" I was thinking of wearing it at a press conference after a game, but eventually thought better of it."

"Bung, Bung You're Dead."
Sun headline after the story Graham had accepted an "unsolicited gift" of £400,000 from agent Rune Hauge to help the transfers of John Jensen and Pal Lydersen broke.

"Hillier did not suggest, incidentally, that he thought the bag was a gift and that, in any case, he intended to give it back at a later date."
Jim White in the Independent, reporting on David Hillier's trial for stealing £3,000 worth of luggage at Gatwick.

"Arsenal FC have now been informed by the FA Premier League Inquiry of the results of their investigations into alleged irregularities concerning certain transfers and the Board have concluded that Mr Graham did not act in the best interests of the club. The Board have therefore terminated Mr Graham's contract as manager."

"I cannot recall a sadder day. For me it was very difficult but George was very calm and sensible about it. I suspect he thought it may be the reason I had asked to see him. It is very sad for me. The saddest for me at the club. I said to George that I was sorry it came to this. We have had some very happy times together and he has been very successful. I speak for everyone on the board when I say that. They have great admiration for what he has achieved and what he stood for."
Peter Hill-Wood, after sacking Graham.

"I deeply regret that this kangaroo court judgement should have been reached in such a hole-in-the-corner way. My record of loyalty and service demanded better treatment. I believe this matter should be fully investigated by the Football Association. What is the future for football if standards of justice inside the game can be ignored in this way?"
An entirely unrepentant Graham's statement after his sacking.

TONY ADAMS

"Tony Adams, I think, is the greatest Arsenal man of all time. On the field, he has to go beyond the likes of Liam Brady and Alex James or Joe Mercer or Frank McLintock. I don't think anyone has represented the club from the age of 17 to the age he is now and sustained the injuries he has, while half of that time he's been fighting his own soul. Only those close to him knew how bad it was."
Bob WIlson.

"I made Tony Adams one of the youngest captains in Arsenal's history and I never had any doubts about him doing the job. The modern game is short of dominant personalities, so Tony stands out like a beacon"
George Graham.

"I remember we lost 4-0 away from home at Maine Road in the 80s, and our fans did the conga around the stand. There were 22,000 hardcore, week in, week out. They are still going, just because it's the Arsenal and they love to go every weekend, but I think the club has accumulated quite a lot of consumers, who, if the steak-and-kidney pie is not good enough they will want a new one."

"Everyone in the Clock End relates to him. But why? Is it because he comes from Essex? Is it because he used to drink himself stupid? Is it because he was sent to prison? Is it because he stopped drinking and started going to the theatre? Is it because he cares enough about his fellow professionals to want to set up a clinic for those who, like him, have addiction problems? Did you relate to him more then, or now?"
Nick Hornby.

"I ... remember a book by Dr Robert Haas. It was called Eat To Win and we had that in 1987, long before Arsene ever came to these shores. Ok, we were drinking 20 pints of lager as well, but we were still eating pasta!"

"Those that say it is the taking part and not the winning that is important are, for me, wrong. It is the other way round."

"A man who has fulfilled every schoolboy's dream. He's won the Double, he's captained England and driven his car into a wall at very high speed. Ladies and gentlemen, Tony Adams."
Adams is introduced to the studio audience of "The Kumars at No. 42."

"I will sign every contract Arsenal put in front of me without reading it."

"I roomed with Tony for ten years and I love him, he's my best mate in football probably. But we went from closing the curtains at seven o'clock and trying to get rid of our hangovers from two days before, to Tony going all scientific! He started reading literature to me and poems and I'd be like 'Tony we've got a big game tomorrow mate and you're reading me a poem, you're supposed to be kicking the players!'"
Ray Parlour.

"I don't actually like people. I'm a loner and if I had my way I'd just walk my dogs every day, never talk to anyone and then die."

"I don't trust anyone who doesn't have self-doubt. But I'm walking tall at the moment. I have a lot of faith in myself and my team. It feels like the right thing to do. Is this too deep for the Daily Mail?"

"For me Arsenal was Tony Adams. He symbolised everything about the Gunners, in terms of his career, his aura, his permanent will to win, in fact in terms of everything he stood for."
Patrick Vieira.

"Fergie said I was a Manchester United player in the wrong shirt – I said he was an Arsenal manager in the wrong blazer."

"My name is Tony and I'm an alcoholic."
Adams comes clean to the dressing room early in the 1996-97 season.

"He's a rubbish alcoholic."
Perry Groves

"It took a lot of bottle for Tony to own up."
Ian Wright's apparently accidental tribute to his captain after he confessed he was an alcoholic.

"The only problem is that now he bores the pants off us with his philosophies, his piano lessons, the plays he has been to see, the books he has read."
David Seaman.

"I realised when I joined Arsenal that the back four were all university graduates in the art of defending and Tony Adams was the doctor of defence."
Arsene Wenger.

"Play for the name on the front of the shirt, and they'll remember the name on the back."
A message apparently lost on Samir Nasri.

"It's my football club, Arsenal Football Club, and when I get an opportunity and if I'm needed and if I'm ready then I'd love to be of service. When I'm needed, when I'm wanted. I'll make the tea there!"

"As far as I'm concerned, Tony is like the Empire State Building."
Ian Wright.

"Tony used to be a cockney but I aint got a clue what he is now."
Jamie "Bow Bells" Redknapp on Adams' reinvention.

"Welcome to hell."
Arsene Wenger in a phone call to Adams after he became Portsmouth manager.

"The average tenure of a club is 1.53 years. There were 34 dismissals in 2007-08. There have been 601 dismissals over the last 15 years. Puts it in perspective, doesn't it?"
Adams to the Guardian's Amy Lawrence in an interview he gave after being named Portsmouth manager. Adams took the job knowing Portsmouth were entering a tailspin and that there was no money for player recruitment. He lasted just 16 matches.

"I would be perfect as a figurehead. Kind of like the statue outside the ground. I would open my arms and greet people, be personable, and always have the best intentions of the club at heart."

"I still feel slightly foreign when I am going to the new stadium, as if I'm going to Paris Saint-Germain."

JOHN LUKIC

"You'd be amazed by the letters I get from solicitors and the like, wanting me to confirm it for their quizzes. There was a Lukic involved, a stewardess I think, but all they have to do to see that it's nonsense is look up my birthdate. If I had a pound for every time it's happened...'
Squashing the rumour that he was a survivor of the Munich air crash because his pregnant mother was supposedly on the plane.

"It wasn't a shock because on deadline day the previous March, he tried to get David and palm me off on loan to QPR. But I declined, and the office staff at Arsenal thanked me the next day. They'd had all this lovely food which was left over from the press conference about David."
After being sold to Leeds.

MARTIN KEOWN

"Keown's got a monkey's head."
Sung by West Ham fans and emblazoned across unofficially produced t-shirts.

"A warrior who put his body on the line every time he played."
Sol Campbell.

'I rang my wife after the game. She's usually very supportive, but she said: "I think you've gone and done it now..."'
After the 0-0 draw at Old Trafford in 2003/04. Even Mrs Keown fell for the pro-United spin.

"Jump up if you hate Manc cheats."
T-shirt on sale outside Highbury a week later, with a picture of Keown jumping above van Nistlerooy.

"'We could have paid for a new roof at the FA for the amount we paid in fines over that incident, but I don't go through my life regretting things."

"This wasn't the only time I was involved in disciplinary matters with him. Whether it was right or wrong, this was pent up. There was a team aggression towards him. He was involved in an incident with Patrick Vieira shortly before the penalty, when he took a dive, feigned injury and Vieira was sent off. It felt like the last straw for this particular individual. We'd had enough of him and any respect went."
On Ruud van Nistlerooy.

"When Arsenal lost the very first game of the season there was mass hysteria – people become unbalanced very quickly."
As a pundit, reflecting on Arsenal's 3-1 opening day loss to Aston Villa in 2013/14.

PAUL DAVIS
"We`d been exchanging words throughout the game, that`s probably how the media would put it. But it was nothing too unusual, until the punch and the next thing I knew I was on the ground."
Glenn Cockerill after Davis broke his jaw in 1988, an assault that earned Davis a nine-match ban.

DAVID ROCASTLE
"Remember who you are, what you are and who you represent."
Rocastle's ethos. This quote is widely attributed to Rocastle, but it was a club mantra drilled into the players by George Graham, Don Howe and Steve Burtenshaw.

"He should have played a million times for England."
Paul Merson.

"David was a top man, who got on equally well with players from his own age range, like Quinny, and Mickey Thomas, or myself and David O'Leary. I'll always remember a happy, streetwise kid, who was confident from the moment he came into the side."
Steve Williams.

"The day I signed for Arsenal, that night I went to his house, and we both stayed up until 4am – talking about Arsenal, the club he loved. He loved that football club so much."
Ian Wright.

"He had everything. He could pass the ball, score goals and take people on. He was also as hard as nails and could really put a tackle in. At the same time he was once of the nicest blokes ever and nobody ever said a bad word about him, which in football was a massive compliment."
Ian Wright.

"I first saw David Rocastle play in 1983 for the youth team. I remember coming home excitedly from the match and telling my family, "I've just watched the nearest thing to a Brazilian footballer you are ever likely to see - and he comes from Lewisham."
David Dein.

"I've lost a very dear friend today."
David O'Leary, on learning of Rocastle's death in 2001.

"There was so much more to Rocky than being a gifted footballer, he was a consummate gentlemen, warm and modest. His genuine sincerity was remarked upon by so many, even those who only met him momentarily."
David Dein.

"David was a true friend, a lovely guy and he is sorely missed. I knew him for years and he never changed one bit. He was one of the genuine men in football and in life."
Tony Adams.

"Rocastle not only had an exceptional dimension as a footballer, but as well a human dimension. Everybody liked him"
Arsene Wenger.

MICHAEL THOMAS

"I remember once when we were doing press-ups at the training ground and Micky wasn't doing them right, according to George. So George actually got on to his back and was trying to make him go right down, but Micky would not give in and he was so stubborn."
Alan Smith.

"I was born and bred in London and I think anybody who's scored the winning goal against any team that cost them the championship would be apprehensive joining that team. I was surprised that Liverpool came in for me. At the time I didn't want to stay in England. I wanted to play abroad. I wanted to go to Italy or Spain but George Graham wouldn't let me go. Liverpool consistently wanted me to come to the club. In the end why would I turn down a great club like Liverpool?"

"Evertonians buy me drinks. Liverpudlians buy me drinks. Everybody buys me drinks."

"They always let me know, even now! There's a lot of banter. It's just a bit of fun. I know it hurts them but they say you paid us back by the goal in the cup final."
Asked if he ever got any grief from Liverpool fans in an interview with LFChistory.net

PAUL MERSON

"He's not a natural goalscorer."
Merson's verdict on the 17-year-old Southampton debutant Alan Shearer before a game at the Dell in 1988. Shearer scored a hat-trick.

"Who the fuck's that?"
"Bloody hell Merse, it's Nelson Mandela."
Nigel Winterburn lets Merson know who he'd just shaken hands with.

"I still haven't a clue what happened in those 72 hours ... whenever a 22-year-old comes up to me these days and asks for an autograph the same thought flashes through my head. 'Please don't call me Dad'."
From Merson's book: "How Not To Be A Professional Footballer."

"No one was twittering or facebooking about me when I was crapping on Spunky's balcony or pushing Grovesey into the sea."

"They haven't got that player around the box with a bit of guile, that can open a can of worms."
Merse as a pundit.

"'Come on Merse, one pint won't kill you.' He was right, but one pint plus another 20 did."
Merson before the opening day defeat to Coventry in 1993-94. Merson played while still drunk after three hours sleep.

"You're a big-nosed French twat."
Merson to David Ginola, during the European Cup Winners Cup semi-final first-leg with PSG in 1993-94, seconds before Ginola scored the equaliser in a 1-1 draw.

"(George Graham) bought the story, apologised for bringing it up and then let me go. Then I went out and scored some more cocaine."
After being called into Graham's office to answer an accusation he'd bought drugs from a pub in Borehamwood.

"Right. We're going to sort you out. We're going to get you help."
Ken Friar's brilliantly Arsenal response when Merson confessed he owed thousands in gambling debts and was addicted to cocaine. The Arsenal secretary was momentarily stunned before regaining his composure.

"If you own a Robin Reliant and it breaks down you get rid of it. If you own a Rolls Royce and it breaks down you get it repaired."
Graham on his reasons for standing behind Merson.

"It wasn't the emotional experience I'd imagined it to be. I just packed my bags and left. There was no leaving party and definitely no champagne."
After being sold to Middlesbrough in 1998.

"Sometimes, on the eve of big games, we would go to a Holiday Inn in Islington where a yellowy product was injected into our arm. In comparison to what I had put in my system, nothing would have scared me."
Merson on a vitamin injection he was given while playing under Arsene Wenger, a story that broke while he publicised his book: "How Not To Be A Professional Footballer" in May 2011.

"If you find one player who I asked to take an injection to play one game, no matter how big the game was, I would resign tomorrow morning. If you find one player who I asked to take something, bring him here in front of me. If we give them something, it is multivitamins, magnesium, calcium or vitamin C like everybody else. Paul Merson stayed with me for four months, so I think it is better you ask people who have played for five, six, seven, eight, nine years here how we behave medically. Do you really think that Paul Merson is convinced that we dope our players? So what was his target? To sell the book."

Wenger's testy reply a day later.

"I'm not saying we shouldn't have a foreign manager, but I think he should definitely be English."
A Merson classic from Soccer Saturday.

PERRY GROVES

"She was attractive, 20 or 21 and a virgin. In that part of the world that's like finding a penny black, I can tell you."
On meeting his wife, Mandy, for the first time.

"I'll take you to the Race Relations Board. You called me a fucking useless ginger twat!"
Turning the tables on a Colchester fan who attended a meeting at Layer Road, expecting Groves to apologise for his response to the initial insult: "The pies are over there - just leave some for someone else!"

"Pure ability and talent is not enough. You need something else. We call it 'arsehole'."

"Rent boy, rent boy, hang him, hang him, hang him!"
Sung to Groves by Millwall fans as he warmed up at the Den.

"You two are mixing with the wrong people."
Graham to Groves and Merson after they'd been caught with Charlie Nicholas and Graham Rix breaking a curfew.

"Chins up big fella."
Groves to Paul Gascoigne after Gazza missed a penalty in front of the North Bank in one of his final games for Newcastle.

"I looked over my shoulder, saw it was a one-on-one and thought Thank God it isn't me."
Groves on Michael Thomas at Anfield.

"Steve, how long to go?"
To Steve "one minute" McMahon.

"I started singing 'my old man, said be a Tottenham fan ...' and the crowd chanted back 'fuck off, bollocks you're a cunt.' I had them in the palm of my hand."
On the balcony of Islington town hall.

"Somehow I got handsomer and sexier every time I progressed up the football ladder. By the time I was in the Gooners side I was Robert Redford."

"Rodders is a rubbish alcoholic. You can't play professional football if you're an alcoholic."
On Tony Adams.

"He joined Arsenal a teetotaler and left a serious drinker."
Paul Merson.

"Perry Groves, what a legend!"
Cesc Fabregas on Twitter, after Groves had suggested Fabregas should join Barcelona. Fabregas's sarcasm was diluted when Fabregas did join Barcelona at the end of that season.

"There were two players that everyone hated playing. Julian Dicks, because he told you exactly what he was going to do to you. And Stuart Pearce, because he didn't say a word, but you knew what he was going to do to you."

"Please release me, let me go."
Groves singing the old Englelbert Humperdink song in training, desperate to join Manchester City so he could play first team football.

"I always believed in having a pair of glasses handy to put on in case there was a fight like that. I couldn't be arsed to get involved either, I thought it was hilarious."
After the first battle of Old Trafford.

"You try and break my legs and I'll put it through yours."
To Oldham defender Andy Barlow, who Groves had nutmegged to set up an Ian Wright equaliser.

"I was in love with Arsenal but Arsenal weren't in love with me anymore."
Realising his Highbury career was over after Jimmy Carter was signed from Liverpool for £500,000. In spite of this Groves and Carter became good friends.

STEVE BOULD

"I was a scorer of great goals. Great own goals."

1-0 DOWN ...

"Do you need any more motivation?"
George Graham to his players, after the half-time 'Spurs are on their way to Wembley!' tannoy announcement at White Hart Lane in 1987.

"Bang out of order."
Perry Groves, on hearing Spurs were already revealing details of Wembley tickets.

ALAN SMITH

"Excuse me referee, are you aware of my disciplinary record?"
Story told by Smith's former Leicester team mate Gary Lineker about Smith's famously even temper. Smith was incredulous the referee felt the need to speak to him.

"I stopped the night there and had contract talks in the morning. But the following day, and just before the talks, I managed to get myself locked in the bathroom. I went for a wash and there was a dodgy handle on the inside of the bathroom. I'm trying to get out, and I am thinking "bloody hell, this is embarrassing", so I had to politely call out and ask for help. Mrs Friar never lets me forget that."
After getting locked in Ken Friar's toilet the night before he signed for Arsenal.

"Sir Alex Ferguson rang me up one day when I was at home to see if I wanted to sign for Manchester United, but I told him that I had already made up my mind to join Arsenal. I wanted to sign for the Gunners because there was just something about them and for those next five years Arsenal were the dominant team and United were lagging so I made the right decision."

"There's only one word for that - straight off the training ground."
During a commentary for Sky.

LEE DIXON

"I used to think my name was 'Stop The Cross!', I heard it so much."

"Extra chips for you lad, I'm an Evertonian!"
A heavily hungover Dixon gets a warm welcome from a chip shop owner, the day after Anfield 89, as recounted by James Curtis of www.arsenalinsider.com

"If I got away from Dixon then I had Keown, if I got away from Keown I had Winterburn. They wanted to destroy me. I wanted to caress the ball but there was no way anyone could do that. Lee Dixon and I laugh about it now but it was not funny at the time, it was frightening. He was like a pitbull, he just wanted to bite me."
David Ginola, talking about the physical and mental scarring he got whenever he played Arsenal.

"We're good mates now, but he still owes me £1,500 for my broken tooth!"
On Ginola.

"I'll see you back here next week after we've given you a good hiding."
To Emmanuel Petit before England's friendly with France in 1999, for which Dixon earned an unexpected call-up. France won 2-0.

"Both teams needed to win and they did."
Dixon on Match of the Day 2, after Arsenal's 2-1 win at Anfield in 2009/10.

BRIAN MARWOOD

"Unless you wiggled your bum at the North Bank, you'd get booed. There was no option."
Marwood on the customary chant of "do the twist" fans sang at players during the warm-up.

ANFIELD 1989

"Don't go out there and try and score two goals in the first 20 minutes. Keep it tight in the first half because if they score first we'll have to get three or four goals at Anfield and that's next to impossible. Get in at half-time with the game 0-0. In the second half you'll go out and score. Then with 15 minutes to go I'll change the team around, they'll shit themselves, you'll have a right old go, score again and win the game 2-0. Ok?"
George Graham's pre-game team talk.

"Great stuff lads, brilliant, perfect. Absolutely outstanding. The plan's going perfectly."
Graham at half-time, to the bewilderment of his players.

"We have laid a foundation of belief at Highbury. If you lose hope, or lose belief, you may as well get out of football. Tonight was the fairy tale, the unpredictable that makes us all love football."

"Look at golden bollocks there. Everything he said came true. He must be a warlock."
Perry Groves.

"There was a lot of fuss about the goal with the Liverpool players surrounding the referee because they thought I was offside or hadn't got a touch to the ball. To be honest, they didn't know what they were appealing for. They thought the linesman's flag had gone up but it hadn't. There was a lot of pressure on the referee, but he pointed to the centre circle and it was game on."
Alan Smith.

"Smith never touched that ball."
Liverpool's Steve Nicol on the same incident.

"I'm going upfield to see if I can pinch a goal."
Thomas to Kevin Richardson a few minutes from full-time at Anfield 89.

"I am thinking "Micky, Micky, shoot. Shoot, Micky" and all the other Arsenal boys are thinking the same.
But Micky was so laid back. He never did anything at anyone else's pace and he just waited, and waited and waited for Bruce Grobbelaar to make his move and go down and that is when he flicked the ball over."
Alan Smith.

"My claim to fame is that my throw-out to Lee Dixon started the move for the stoppage-time goal. I was at the Kop end and wasn't sure how they'd react to me leaping about, so I decided to be constrained - then went mad afterwards.'
John Lukic.

"Thomas, charging through the midfield... it's up for grabs now... Thomas, right at the end!"
Brian Moore, ITV's commentator.

"It's like an out of body experience."
Thomas, reflecting on the moment in the documentary "It's Up For Grabs Now!"

DAVID SEAMAN

"I think John Lukic is one of the best three goalkeepers in the country. I just think David Seaman is the best."
George Graham after signing Seaman from QPR in 1990.

"He is a truly magnificent keeper. I am lucky to play in front of him every week. You look

over your shoulder and feel safe."
Tony Adams.

"They couldn't really call me spunky when the younger fans are around. So they settled on H. It's cockney rhyming slang: Harry Monk - spunk."
Seaman on how he got his nickname in his autobiography, "Safe Hands."

"Merse and I got in the bath at Wembley and were pissing ourselves. We thought it was funny to see H blubbing."
Perry Groves on differing reactions to the 1991 FA Cup semi-final defeat. Seaman blamed himself for two of the goals.

"That Seaman is a handsome young man but he spends too much time looking in his mirror, rather than at the ball. You can't keep goal with hair like that."
Brian Clough.

ANDERS LIMPAR

"It will make me go quicker."
Explaining why he shaved off all his body hair.

COLIN PATES

"Nothing personal? Putting stones in my foreskin? I'm woken up by a hotel receptionist with my trousers round my ankles and stones in my foreskin. Not personal?"
Pates after falling asleep and suffering a practical joke, which he was told was "nothing personal."

DAVID HILLIER

"The rush is incredible: football just can't compare. It's the fear factor kicking in. Anyone who's been a fireman will tell you that you can't appreciate what it's like - not being able to see a thing, you can't breathe, it's very claustrophobic. It may look like a big house from the outside, but inside it's just full of smoke and you haven't a clue where you're going. When you're confronting a big fire it gets bloody hot as well. I've been in rooms that have been anything up to 1000 degrees at the top."
On becoming a fireman after retiring from football.

"The player threw himself at the magistrate's mercy, saying that he was distraught at his stupidity and that his form had dipped to such a degree since the incident, what with all the guilt and worrying, that he was now on the transfer list. The magistrate accepted his plea, although a closer observer of the game would have pointed out that it wasn't necessarily the crime: anybody's form would suffer if they were obliged to share the midfield with John Jensen and Martin Keown."
Jim White of the Independent reporting on the court case during which Hillier was found guilty of taking another passengers luggage at Gatwick.

"The most underrated player I ever played with."
Ian Wright.

THE TUESDAY CLUB

"The pint-o-meter usually came in at 15 beers plus."
Paul Merson.

"I was still gambling and my drinking was on the increase. It's really strange how well I was still able to play. In fact it was a bloody marvel most of us were able to play. In fact it was a bloody marvel most of us were able to play as well as we did, given the drink culture that was growing at an alarming rate."
Kenny Sansom.

"I'll always remember the moment Steve Bould went up to the bar and ordered 35 pints for five of us. After we left the bar we spotted all the French lads in the coffee shop and they were sitting around smoking, I thought how are we going to win the league this year? We're all drunk and they're all smoking, and we ended up winning the double that year."
Ray Parlour, on Arsenal's first pre-season tour under Arsene Wenger, in an interview with Sportlobster TV.

"We would head down the road to the Bank of Friendship pub outside the ground. We'd have a couple of pints of Guinness and then head into town. Some of the lads stretched it into Wednesday, but that was the culture at the time and it is amazing to look back at it now. Drinking to that extent is not good for your fitness. It is ruinous. We had this idea that you could sweat it out on a Thursday."
Alan Smith.

"On a Monday, Wednesday and Thursday people were dressed in tracksuits. On a Tuesday everyone turned up with their suits on, George was trying to work out was going on – but we were obviously going out on the town."
Ray Parlour.

"You are banned! You are not coming out with the Tuesday club again!"
Merson to Jimmy Carter, after he passed out at 5.45pm, having already pissed on both Merson and Perry Groves' trousers.

"It was a strain for me at the start because if you didn't drink, you didn't conform and people thought there was something wrong with you. It was a bit difficult really to turn my back on that culture, but I didn't feel I'd come to London to waste my money drinking."
Martin Keown.

"Imagine how much fitter you would be if you did not drink!"
Non-member Anders Limpar.

"It all stopped really when Arsene Wenger put a ban on drink being served in the lounge, and then Tony (Adams) gave up drinking."
Nigel Winterburn.

IAN WRIGHT

'I want Arsenal to have the very best players in all positions and when good ones come along you try to buy them.' 'The fees are not important to me. Getting the best team and the best players is my business.'
George Graham after signing Wright for £2.5 million from Crystal Palace.

"When I signed for Arsenal, the fans and media were like, 'What are they buying him for?' I remember watching TV the night I signed, and they were all saying, "He's not good enough to play for Arsenal." And I remember just sitting there – literally shitting myself."

"John McGinlay? Fuck off!"
Wright to Bruce Rioch, after Rioch told him the Bolton striker would have scored one of the chances Wright missed.

"I was once fined £5,000 for calling Coventry fans wankers. Best £5,000 I ever spent."

"I love him to death."
Glenn Hoddle.

"(He) was dancing away to Michael Jackson. Arsene was looking at Ian strutting his stuff and, because I had joined before him, he turned to me and asked if Wright was like that after every game."
Patrick Vieira on Wright's dancing.

"He once shanked a shot so badly that he shouted, 'I need to self-harm!' then drove his buggy into a tree. Unfortunately, I was in the buggy, and he jumped out to safety. I was the one who got hurt."
Lee Dixon, after a round of golf with Wright.

"He took his trousers off and put them on the driver's head ... the driver slammed on the breaks violently and Ian was thrown forward against the windscreen, to general laughter."
Emmanuel Petit.

WREXHAM

"Why don't you taffs give us a game? We've come all the way from London for this?"
Ian Wright, winding up the Wrexham fans at half-time.

"Blimey, that's got a chance."
Perry Groves, in the split second the free-kick from Mickey Thomas flew over his head for the equaliser.

"I live off now what happened on that day because they were the reigning league champions and Wrexham had finished bottom of the league in the previous season. It's great for me personally and it brings back great memories. I've never got sick and tired of talking about that goal or that game even though it's not too kind on Arsenal. I don't care what anyone else says, it is for me the greatest ever FA Cup shock. We were playing the champions of England so the gulf in class was immense."
Mickey Thomas in 2012.

"George didn't say much either. It was a case of 'get changed and on the coach quickly so we can get the f*** out of here'. He, like the rest of us, felt it was a day to forget but on the way home our coach broke down and we all had to stand around on the hard shoulder until a replacement came, so it was a nightmare all round."
Alan Smith, for once in his life resorting to bad language.

ANDY LINIGHAN

"I was in the treatment room once the day after a game. Swollen ankle. The manager comes in and he wanted me out of the club. He says to me, Norman Hunter used to play with those."
At Leeds, where he got little sympathy from Billy Bremner.

"I never thought of taking him off. It's nothing to worry about, it gives the face character."
George Graham, after Linighan's injury time winner against Sheffield Wednesday in 1993. Linighan played through the pain of a broken nose after he was elbowed by Wednesday's Mark Bright.

"It was getting tasty, Tony (Adams) had gone through the back of someone and John Jensen put Chris Waddle up in the air. Then I jump with Mark Bright – elbow on the nose."
Linighan's version of that incident.

"Danny Wilson takes this shot and it hit my finger right on the tip. It snapped at a right angle to the rest of my fingers. I'm thinking, 'Hang on, look at my finger'. Awful. But you have the adrenaline. I used to dream about Wembley as a boy."
Linighan played for all but the first 15 minutes of the replay with a serious finger injury.

JOHN JENSEN

"I got a shock when I realised what the fans were expecting when I joined. The harder I tried to score, the worse it got. Every time I gathered the ball the cry would go up 'shoot, shoot, shoot'. It was crazy."

"John says to me, 'Big man, it was going for the top corner.'"
Andy Linighan, on the shot that earned the last-minute corner in the 1993 FA Cup final replay, from which Linighan scored.

"I'll be there when Jensen scores."
A song which evolved into "I'll be dead when Jensen scores."

"I saw Jensen score for Arsenal"
T-shirt printed after Jensen's one and only goal for Arsenal, in a 3-1 defeat at home to QPR in the 1994/95 season.

"I will never forget the noise when I finally did score. The cheering just went on and on."

"They were coming up to me later, mobbing me, showing me their T-shirts. I dedicated my goal to Arsenal and all those fans who, in the end, made me feel so wanted and made my time, in a strange sort of way, so enjoyable."

"Even after I left I kept getting messages of support, telling me they would never forget me. It felt strange to be such a phenomenon when, really, I had failed them in their expectations of me."

THE 1993 FA CUP FINAL
ARSENAL 2 SHEFFIELD WEDNESDAY 1

"What an initially grotesque match... for much of the time this occasion was an unmitigated disgrace. It is sad that Sheffield Wednesday, who have played with distinction for much of the season, have been sucked down over a series of three matches at Wembley, to the same expedient level as Arsenal."
David Miller of The Times.

PAUL DICKOV

"An upstart Jock midget, all 5"6 of him... he was a lookalike for Ali Campbell from the band UB40. And he'd done fuck all in the game."
Perry Groves, after Dickov told Geordie Armstrong to "fuck off".

RAY PARLOUR

"I'd put on a Red shirt and run through brick walls for Arsenal."

"There is a buuurrrmm."
To Arsene Wenger in the corridor at Selhurst Park, after a floodlight failure during a Wimbledon v Arsenal 1997-98.

"Short back and sides please..."
The remark Parlour made to faith healer Eileen Drewery - which allegedly resulted in his exclusion from England's squad for France 1998.
"In fairness she laughed," Parlour said later, in Drewery's defence. "But she told her husband and it was suddenly in The Sun! I never got picked for England again." (In fact he did get picked, but not by Hoddle.

"To me, he will always be the Romford Pele."
Marc Overmars.

"I can understand everyone apart from Ray Parlour."
Junichi Inamoto, Arsenal's first Japanese player.

"It's only Ray Parlour."
Tim Lovejoy in Sky's fanzone, seconds before parlour scored from 25-yards in the 2002 FA Cup Final.

'I'll always remember the first pre-season tour with Arsene Wenger. New French lads had come into the team like Patrick Vieira, Emmanuel Petit and Gilles Grimandi. We worked our socks off and at the end of the trip Wenger said we could all go out. 'You know what we were like, we went straight down to the pub and the French lads went to the coffee shop."

"He's in a cave somewhere having the time of his life, mate. Surrounded by women, having a right laugh. Probably plotting."
Parlour, quoted in 4-4-2 in 2008, on the wherabouts of Osama Bin Laden.

Once, we were in a hotel, and Arsene Wenger went up to the dessert trolley whilst everybody is sitting down as normal. He's got the spatula out with his Apple Pie, and as he has turned around, the pie fell off his plate. And you talk about he doesn't see a lot – but he didn't see his Apple Pie fall off his plate I'm telling you! So he's walked through all of the players, with everybody smiling, watching and waiting. He finally sits down at his table, gets his spoon out, looks down, and says, 'Where's my Apple Pie?'"

"What an honour. I'm pleased, because I wasn't one of those players who stick out and do magical things every game, but I think they liked how I worked."
After being voted the 19th greatest ever Arsenal player in a survey conducted by www.arsenal.com

"I feel very privileged to have played with such great players and proud to have played for Arsenal. I wish I could still play; I miss the banter in the dressing room – we had such a fantastic spirit. We got on well as a team and I loved every minute of it."

BRUCE RIOCH

"I really let him down and so did Merse. And I've said sorry to Bruce, but I was spending more time in the pub than I was on the training ground."
Tony Adams.

"I feel like Marje Proops with you lot."
Comparing himself to the Daily Mirror agony aunt after a pre-season friendly with Ipswich, shortly before his dismissal.

"Every time (the ball) went through his legs the lads would shout 'ole!' They would keep this up until he cracked and took one of the players out with a wicked tackle."
David Seaman on Rioch's unsuccessful strategy for imposing his authority on the Arsenal squad.

"We'd respected George for so long, and then Rioch comes in with his iron rod and starts smacking us with 'now you're gonna do it this way'. I ended up in the reserves long before Wenger."
David Hillier to the Guardian.

DENNIS BERGKAMP

"If Ryan Giggs is worth £20 million, Denis Bergkamp is worth £100 million."
Marco van Basten

"We get the BBC in Holland so I know all about teletext. I call up Page 301 and I'm shocked. The first two lines are in huge letters. BERGKAMP JOINS ARSENAL. ... I'm in this strange city where I drive on the left and ... I'm on teletext!"

"Annoyingly often I was told I should do something about it. People would say 'you can take a course to cure it you know?' That really pissed me off… It got so bad I would look up at the sky during away games to see what the weather was like. Were there any clouds coming? Sometimes I was preoccupied by the last flight home while I was playing football. It was hell."
On his fear of flying.

"Spurs was mentioned and that had been Hoddle's team, but even then I considered Arsenal to be a bit above Spurs. I'm not sure why."

"I saw Highbury for the first time … wow! This was football. I loved all the houses around but, then you turn the corner and there's the stadium."

"Who'd put their car in a fucking stupid place like this? So I get out of my car to tell him what I think of his parking and he gets out of his car … and it's Dennis Bergkamp! … He's being literally zen-master cool and I'm screaming because I've been praying that it's true that Dennis Bergkamp is going to sign for Arsenal. And here he is!"
Ian Wright, after a chance meeting with Bergkamp at Clackett Lane services..

"Arsenal have wasted their money on Dennis Bergkamp. We've got a better player for less money in Chris Armstrong."
Alan "Lord" Sugar.

HARTLE-FOOL
Tabloid headline after Bergkamp failed to score against Hartlepool in a league cup tie.

"Normally a player will have nothing on. And Dennis comes out in full pyjamas! … It was so lovely. PYJAMAS!"
Ian Wright on his new room mate's dressing habits at night.

"What a waste of money."
Sung by more than one set of opposition supporters.

"That moment was the start of my relationship with the Arsenal crowd. They'd been patient with me and I don't know why … after that goal we never lost that relationship."
On his first goal for Arsenal in a 4-2 win over Southampton.

"He's the messiah. We told him to get us into Europe when he joined and that's exactly what he did."
Ian Wright.

"I started clapping myself until I realized that I was Sunderland's manager."
Peter Reid after a typical Bergkamp goal v Sunderland in the FA Cup 3rd round, 1996-97. Arsenal won 2-0 at Roker Park.

"A very good player, but a shit man."
Frank Leboeuf, after Arsenal had beaten Chelsea 3-2 at Stamford Bridge in 1997-98.

"Dennis is the best player I have ever played with as a partner. It is a dream for a striker to have him in the team with you."
Thierry Henry.

"Dennis was disappointed not to be here but he didn't want to travel by train, either. Perhaps trains are too fast for him as well."
Wenger on Bergkamp's refusal to even board a train to a Champions League game at Lyon in 2000-01.

"When Dennis Bergkamp scores, it's not a common goal, it's always what we call 'a Dennis Bergkamp goal'."
Henry.

"Intelligence and class. Class is of course, most of the time linked to what you can do with the ball, but the intelligence makes you use the technique in an efficient way. It's like somebody who has a big vocabulary but he doesn't say intelligent words, and somebody who has a big vocabulary but he can talk intelligently, and that's what Dennis is all about. What he does, there's always a head and always a brain. And his technique allows him to do what he sees, and what he decides to do."
Wenger.

"When I played in Holland, I always tried to lob the goalkeeper. People used to say, 'Oh, you're always only trying to make a nice goal'. But I said, 'listen, if the goalie is a little bit off his line, how much space do you have on his left or right? It's not a lot. And how much space do you have above him? There is more. It's a question of mathematics."

"Everything depends on whether Bergkamp plays."
"I didn't know he was injured."
"He isn't. I said it depends on whether he plays, really plays."
An exchange between a Dutch journalist and Johan Neeskens, before Holland's World Cup semi-final with Brazil in 1978. Neeskens was referring to Bergkamp's tendency to go missing from games.

"Ten yards before the ball arrived I made my decision: I'm going to turn him. I knew where Dabizas was. The thought was, 'just flick the ball and see what happens'. Maybe he'll block it, or the flick won't be wide enough, or he'll anticipate and get two yards ahead. Or maybe he'll be surprised and I'll be one or two yards in front of him. As it happened, I still wasn't in front of him, so I had to push him off. So you need some luck as well."
Describing his goal at Newcastle in 2001-02.

"He was fantastic. Like a dancer."
Kolo Toure.

"I really like Arsenal. But you, do you like Arsenal? Or just Arsenal with Trophies?"
Bergkamp, several years after his retirement, questioning the loyalty of gloryhunting fans.

DAVID PLATT

"He never slept! ... He was always on his laptop conducting business. I would try to get some sleep but all I could hear was the sound of him tapping away on the keyboard. ... Eventually I had to have my own room."

Patrick Vieira.

PART FOUR
1996 ONWARDS

ARSENE WENGER

"Daily life can drag you down. Football can be a fantastic experience for people."

"There is no better psychological education than growing up in a pub because when you are five or six years old, you meet all different people and hear how cruel they can be to each other. From an early age you get a practical, psychological education to get into the minds of people."

"He is a hybrid. He is highly intelligent – he speaks five or six languages. He is cool, calm and collected, a great tactician. He also knows a lot about medicine. It's very rare that you find all that in a manager."
David Dein.

"I was the best ... in my village."
On his playing career.

"When you let four in you keep your trap shut."
Guy Roux, after Wenger reacted sourly when his Monaco lost 4-1 to Roux's Auxerre.

"I bet it's fucking Arsene Wenger because I haven't heard of him."
Fever Pitch author Nick Hornby, admitting he hadn't expected much when Wenger was first appointed.

"I tried to watch the Tottenham match on television in my hotel yesterday, but I fell asleep."
A (successful) early attempt to win over the Arsenal faithful.

"If something comes out that is not correct I will attack."
Facing down journalists at Highbury in 1996 after false and malicious rumours were circulated about him when he was named Arsenal manager.

"He looked a bit like a geography teacher."
Lee Dixon, on his initial impression of the new manager.

"By the time we'd finished our first training session I knew that life at Arsenal would never be the same again. The bloke was a genius."
Paul Merson.

"When Arsene came to Arsenal he took complete control of our diets. We were allowed no salt, no fat and no sugar, in the end you wanted to play a team like Millwall so that someone would throw a banana at you just so you could have something to eat."
Ian Wright.

"I remember I took away the chocolate bars and the players were singing 'we want our chocolate back'."

"Mr Wenger has passed up the opportunity to be a gentleman."
Ginaluca Vialli after a 3-1 defeat at Chelsea in a League Cup semi-final in 1998.

"If you eat caviar every day it's difficult to return to sausages."
After a grim 1-1 draw with Middlesbrough in 1998-99, when a last-minute goal from Anelka spared Arsenal from an embarrassing defeat.

"Everyone thinks they have the prettiest wife at home."
Rebutting Alex Ferguson's claim that Manchester United had played the best football in the 2001-02 season.

"What I don't understand is that he does what he wants and you are all at his feet."
Accusing the media of double standards re Ferguson.

"Perhaps he sent it by horse."
Asked if he had received an apology from "Sir" Alex.

"I don't drink alcohol, it destroys people. If you put the wrong fuel in a car it won't go very far."

"I think in England you eat too much sugar and meat and not enough vegetables."

"Sometimes I see it but I say that I didn't see it to protect the players and because I could not find any rational explanation for that they did."
On his infamously selective vision.

"Can you buy players at Waitrose? It's not a supermarket, you can only use the transfer market you have."
On his reluctance to spend money on players.

"When I arrive at the gates of Heaven the Good Lord will ask 'what did you do in your life?' I will respond 'I tried to win football matches.' He will say: 'Are you certain that's all?' But, well, that's the story of my life."

"It's like a child who is used to having ice cream whenever he wants. When it doesn't come when he asks he tends to get confused and nervous."
On Arsenal's support, after a disappointing 1-1 draw at Crystal Palace, 2004-05.

"Give me the names of the world class players who are available."
On his failure to spend money during one of many frustrating transfer windows.

"They are a financially doped club. They have enhancement of performances through financial resources which are unlimited. It puts pressure on the market that is not very healthy. They can go to Steven Gerrard or Rio Ferdinand and say 'how much do you earn? We'll give you twice as much'. I don't know if there is anything we can do to stop it."
When asked about Chelsea during a press conference for the 2005 FA Cup Final.

"Fuck off."
To Alan Pardew after being goaded about a last-minute winner for West Ham at Upton Park in 2006-07.

"This guy should never play football again. What is he doing on the football pitch? I've gone along with the idea for a long time that to stop Arsenal, you have to kick Arsenal. I knew that was coming for a long time now."
Wenger on Martin Taylor, after the tackle that snapped Eduardo's leg, 2007-08.

"The penalty decision was Old Traffordish."
After a 2-1 defeat in 2009-10. With Arsenal leading 1-0, United were awarded a penalty after Rooney "anticipated" a challenge by Almunia and went down before contact was made.

"Spare me the articles about how nice Shawcross is because that was a horrendous tackle. People say we don't fancy the physical side of it, but this is the result. If you see a player getting injured like that, it's not acceptable."
Wenger after Ryan Shawcross's equally horrific tackle on Aaron Ramsey in 2009-10.

"At the start of his career he reacted more and he showed emotions more. He has learnt to control his reactions. He has learnt that it's no use throwing tantrums except for now and then."
Jean-Luc Arribart, one of Wenger's players at Nancy.

"I have never seen him like that. Maybe he should do it more often."
Cesc Fabregas after Wenger threw one of his very rare tantrums at half-time at Anfield. Arsenal responded by coming from 1-0 down to win 2-1.

"Am I suggesting there were a lot of bad tackles? Leave me alone with that, for fuck's sake. You are always looking for controversy, you do not need me to tell you what happened on the pitch. I can give you my opinion about our game but you always create this controversy."
After a 1-1 draw at Birmingham, when for the second time in three years a title-chasing Arsenal side had been denied the win by a last-minute goal. Wenger was incensed by some of the tackling.

"We still have not found a machine who can measure the intensity of love. We would all buy it."
On Theo Walcott's commitment to Arsenal, August 2012.

"What's hard is that feeling that something is coming to an end. You had a project with guys you had bought at 18 and who left at 23. That's not what you dreamed of."
On the summer of 2011.

"You forget what you wrote last September, October, November. You have a little bit of Alzheimer's."
Wenger to the press corps after a 0-0 draw at Aston Villa.

"A football team is like a beautiful woman. When you do not tell her, she forgets she is beautiful."

"I never go out 48 hours before the game. For dinner, anything, just prepare for the game. You have to sacrifice your life in this job. If you want to do it like I did for 30 years, without stopping, ever, you have to be prepared to work seven days a week, and the whole year."

"Every defeat is a scar on your heart, that remains for life."
To ITV, in an interview given before the 2014 FA Cup Final.

PATRICK VIEIRA

"We were lucky compared to others in the neighbourhood because we had a TV. Not many of us did."
Vieira on his early years in Senegal, where he was one of the few Arsenal players to experience genuine poverty.

"I had the impression that other people thought I was a cheat and I have never cheated when it comes to football."
On rumours he was older than the age on his birth certificate while playing youth football for FC Drouais.

"Suddenly (Claude) Puel looked like a kid compared to him. I immediately told myself that this Vieira guy would one day be a great player. It had taken 45 minutes of a league cup fixture to convince me."
Arsene Wenger, on the first time he saw Vieira play for Cannes against Monaco in a French League Cup tie.

"It was almost like being kidnapped."
After signing for AC Milan. Vieira was flown from Cannes to Milan in a private jet before signing a contract in a language, Italian, that he didn't understand.

"I told David Dein he should not hesitate about the signing because if he wanted Vieira to come to the club he had to act quickly, otherwise he would lose him."
Wenger on perhaps his best ever transfer deal for Arsenal, before he'd even officially become their manager in 1996.

"In order to win the ball from Patrick Vieira in 1996 it didn't take one man, it didn't take two, it took at least three men around him. And even those couldn't be sure of winning the ball. He was huge for me, immediately."
Wenger.

"When all the English teams saw this giant who was crunching into everyone the whole time they couldn't believe their eyes. When players had a go at him he gave as good as he got and when they had a go at him the second time he would make sure he returned the favour three times. And the English loved that immediately!"
Wenger.

"I realised I must have come to the right club if a man - the captain - could stand up in front of his friends and team mates and tell them about something like this."
On realising Tony Adams had just admitted to being an alcoholic. Vieira hadn't understood a word of Adams' confessional speech in the dressing room.

"He's such a monster. It's like tackling two blokes."
Sir Bobby Robson.

"The English are passionate about football in a healthy manner. In Italy it's different and more complicated. If you are doing well you are the king of the castle, everyone welcomes you with open arms; if however you lose two or three games, people start to throw stones at you."

"For the price of my house in London I could buy a house in Paris with an indoor and outdoor pool."

"Every year we told ourselves that we were going to feel the heat during the summer because there would be pressure on us and we would end up selling him. We're not a club with infinite resources. So on the one hand it was a fantastic feeling to have a player like him and the other it was a bit concerning as well."
Wenger on the transfer speculation that surfaced every summer over Vieira's future.

"He told me something that, without shocking me, still haunts me to this day and, I think, always will ... Compared to a player like Emmanuel Petit who had involved himself completely in the training sessions and during all the friendly games, I had shown less commitment."
On realising he wasn't a first-choice for the French 98 World Cup team.

"In private Patrick is a quiet guy. He knows as well as I do, that there are no real friends in this job. We all have an ego problem, linked to competition. Some times our interests are the same as our friends. We can equally find ourselves in competition for club or country."
Emmanuel Petit.

"Hundreds of United fans invaded the pitch ... Most of them gathered by the tunnel and one went up to Patrick, effing and blinding right in his face. Patrick thumped him out of the way and when the fan complained to a policeman who had seen what happened he told him he deserved what he'd got and to get lost."
David Seaman, after the 1999 FA Cup semi-final defeat.

"He missed me but it was close enough to smell the garlic on his breath."
Neil Ruddock after Vieira spat at him following a sending off at Upton Park. Ruddock goaded Vieira as he walked off the pitch but managed to avoid an FA charge for racism.

"We have to ensure that the provocateurs are judged in the same light as the people they provoke. For me what Ruddock said after the game was more shocking even than what he did on the field."
Wenger.

"What he said in the interview was only minor. I am a Frenchman and I don't like garlic. You can call me a French so and so and I don't think it is racial."
Wenger on the same incident, after some reflection.

"Sometimes on the field we could find each other with our eyes shut. Once we were separated, after 2000, I don't think either of us ever found the same level."
Petit.

"I hear stuff after the game, I know that some players in the other team are told their job during the game is to wind me up. I feel sorry for managers who feel they have to do that."
After another red card, this time after a 2-0 win over Liverpool in the second game of the 2000-01 season. Vieira had already been sent off in the season opener at Sunderland.

"Ironically it was not a dirty game ..."
BBC report from the same game, a match which saw Vieira, Didi Hamann and Gary McAllister all sent off.

"You are never really fully fit. You have to learn to live with it, to train and to win with it."
On injuries.

"I was 24 years old and in terms of my international career I had already won all there was to win. But you always want to do better."

"Appeal Patrick."
Roy Keane to Vieira after his sending off at Old Trafford in the 2003/04 season.

"As professional players, given our status, there are some things we shouldn't allow ourselves to do. But people must also forget that we are also human and that we each have our own way of reacting to situations, depending on our feelings and emotions at the time. It was the injustice that made us behave as we did and that's a feeling that we have experienced all too often when we have played against Manchester United."
On the same game.

"Watch it because I'm going to land one on you."
Vieira to Ruud van Nistlerooy after the match. Vieira blamed the Dutchman for his dismissal.

"At the end of Euro 2004 there had been a persistent rumour that the Gunners allegedly held a supernatural hold over the international team. That particularly irritated me."

"I'd have gone to war with that man... ."
Ashley Cole (Meaning, presumably, that he'd go to war alongside Vieira rather than fight him).

"We are neutral."
David Dein to Vieira on Juventus's approach in 2005. Vieira said this was the moment he realised, with a certain amount of anger, that Arsenal wanted to get rid of him.

REMI GARDE

"I have rarely seen a player who has such little confidence in himself transmit so much confidence in others."
Arsene Wenger.

At the first training sessions we said to Raymond (Domenech, the coach) if he doesn't break anything, that's something."
Bernard Lacombe, sporting director of Lyon on Garde's fitness record.

NICOLAS ANELKA

"A wanker."
Unnamed member of the Arsenal first team squad when asked what Anelka was 'really like'.

"I like group life and I've never had a problem with blending in, but I hate it when people decide things for me. He thought I would wisely obey him. It didn't work like that with me. I'm a Parisian and proud of it, but I had something to say. I want to decide what I do with my life so I decided to leave for Arsenal."
The 17-year-old Anelka, feeling disrespected by PSG's sporting director Jean-Michel Moutier, explains his reasons for the first of many moves.

"Overmars, Bergkamp and Petit used to hit me with long balls of diabolical precision, absolutely incomparable, I never again found such a quality of passing."
In his autobiography.

I don't care if they're French or Dutch or Taiwanese. If they're good, and they want to play for Arsenal (hello, Nicolas!), they're welcome.
Nick Hornby.

"I'd just done the double with Arsenal and I still don't understand his reasons for leaving me out. He just said, 'You, I'm not taking you. It's normal'. Nothing else. Those words will stay with me for the rest of my life."
On being left out of France's 1998 World Cup squad. Anelka didn't bother watching the final.

"The Incredible Sulk"
Nickname given to Anelka by the British tabloid press.

"There was only one problem and that was Nicolas."
David Seaman on rumours of a rift between the English and foreign players in the Arsenal dressing room.

"I hope Nicolas remembers that no matter how much money you have, you still only eat three times a day and sleep in one bed. But you can miss a career."
Arsene Wenger.

"Nicholas Anelka left Arsenal for 23 million and they built a training ground on him."
Kevin Keegan.

"What has he ever won? One French title with Lyon, and with that team any coach from the division d'honneur could have won it."
Anelka, building bridges with French coach Jacques Santini.

"He'd have to get down on his knees before me, say sorry first of all and then I'll think about it."
On what it would take for him to consider an international recall from Santini.

"When he left here he was a regular in the national team, just ahead of Euro 2000. He left, Thierry Henry came here and played in the European Championship. He was never accepted at Real Madrid, went back to Paris St Germain and it was always up and down for him after that. He had so much class and is now back to the top level, but he wanted to come back here. I considered it because he wanted to put it right."
Wenger, having toyed with the idea of buying Anelka back in 2007. Anelka joined Chelsea instead.

"You don't know what you're doing."
Chelsea crowd to Avram Grant after he brought Anelka on as sub during a pivotal game in the title race between Chelsea and Arsenal at Stamford Bridge. Anelka set up one goal and scored another as Chelsea came from 1-0 down to win 2-1.

"That's out of the question."
Anelka to Avram Grant when asked if he would take a penalty in the 2008 Champions League final shoot-out. He subsequently relented, but missed.

"I was asked to take one of the first five kicks, but I said: 'That is out of the question, I have come on basically as a right back and you want me to take a penalty.' So I had to go in seventh, but Van der Sar pushed away my shot. All the better for him, that is the game."

"Of all four national team coaches that I've worked with, I have the best relationship with him."
Anelka on Raymond Dommenech before the 2010 World Cup.

"I know he's unpopular, but I can assure you he's a fun guy ... I'm not one of his mates, but he knows he can count on me."
On Dommenech again.

"Go fuck yourself you dirty son of a whore!"
Quote attributed to Anelka, supposedly said to Dommenech during the during the 2010 World Cup. The quote was subsequently splashed all over the front page of L'equipe. Anelka sued the newspaper and lost.

"The so-called punishment has no relevance whatsoever because, for me, the French national team was an issue which ended on June 19 when I was kicked out of the training centre at Knysna. This is just to entertain the public, to turn the page because Laurent Blanc needs to be able to work in peace. These people are clowns. I am dying with laughter."
After receiving the 18-match ban that effectively ended his international career.

"Following the quotes which were attributed to me today in a British newspaper, I would like to categorically deny having given any interview, let alone discussed my future. I am under contract with Chelsea until the end of the season, with many playing commitments."
Anelka talking to AFP in November 2011. Two months before moving to China.

"Wishing to retain my integrity, I have therefore taken the decision to free myself"
After being sacked by West Brom for making an anti-semitic "quenelle" gesture

EMMANUEL PETIT

"L'emmerdeur."
Arsene Wenger's nickname for Petit at Monaco.

"At Monaco you're already playing without the public behind you. If there are guys scuttling you in your own dressing room it's no longer possible."
On finding out some of his Monaco team mates had accepted bribes to throw a match with Marseilles.

"At the end of our meeting I asked Tottenham's representatives if they could order me a taxi. In fact I had to get to Arsene Wenger's house because I had a meeting with him."
Confirming the story that Spurs had paid for him to get to Wenger's house was true.

"By saying you don't deserve your place you're making me look like a cunt. You shouldn't doubt yourself to others. Everyone is responsible for their own career so it's up to you to prove that I wasn't wrong."
French manager Michel Platini to Petit after the latter had questioned whether the former should have handed him an international call-up.

"He's blonde, he's quick, his name is porno slick."
What Petit thought Arsenal fans were singing to him.

"I'd like to be remembered like Ian Wright or Cantona, both are mad and people like these two make the world progress. Eric and his charisma showed everyone you can be a mug, a talented, generous player... and French! I refused to attend many TV shows, both in England and France, I couldn't see any interest in it... I accepted Ian's invitation because I love this guy."
On why he agreed to go on Ian Wright's chat show.

"Don't laugh, but he wants to know what position you play."
Barcelona reserve keeper, translating for his manager Lorenzo Serra Ferrer, after Petit completed his move from Highbury.

"If I have one regret it's leaving Arsenal for Barcelona. I saw this separation as a break-up, like the end of a love story when you know it's all over but despite everything wish the other party would make the effort to stay with you."

"He's a very, very insecure boy, I think, deep down. I think he's misunderstood, very misunderstood. I think his ability is phenomenal. Defensively he was fantastic, he knew

how to play, he had a good football brain, he could pass the ball I'm going to miss him. I wanted him to play for Arsenal and I think it's unfortunate he's not playing now."
Tony Adams

"I had the feeling that I was an ex-Gunner at the Blues. I felt it in my relationship with the fans and with certain players like John Terry and Frank Lampard, who were dreaming of one thing: reaching the summits I had reached. Was it ambition or jealousy? I don't really know, but in any case I never really felt at home at Chelsea."

"When he came to visit us at our training camp I had the impression he was like a mafia boss surrounded by his bodyguards. His attitude disturbed me. I couldn't help thinking that by investing in Chelsea he was buying his respectability and impunity. I don't think for one moment that his motivation was anything to do with a love of the sport."
On Roman Abramovich.

"I allowed myself to dream in secret that my knee would get better, that I would play for Arsenal again and beat Chelsea."
On an abortive attempt at a comeback with Arsenal in 2004. Petit was forced to retire.

GILLES GRIMANDI

"A French Gus Caesar."
Contributor to the Gooner.

"We will never win the league with the likes of Gilles Grimandi in the side and that is an undeniable fact."
Contributor to an Arsenal fanzine, three months before Arsenal won the double - with Grimandi in the side.

"France win Euro 2000 - without The Grimster."
Headline from the sadly defunct website www.grimster.co.uk

"It was not a punch. I caught him with the flat of my hand because I was trying to push him away when he pulled my shirt and held me as we went in for a free-kick being taken. It was not my intention to hurt him even though throughout the match I was being hit all the time."
After punching Diego Simeone during Arsenal's 1-1 draw with Lazio in 2000-01.

"At the start of the game, when we shook hands, the Lazio players were spitting in our faces and making racist remarks to Patrick Vieira. It was disgusting behaviour. I thought we handled ourselves very well."
After the same game.

"Two or three seconds later I thought why did you react like that. I react too quickly. Off the pitch I don't like fights, I'm not aggressive, but it's my personality in football. I got two or three red cards at Monaco as well. Sometimes opposing players are not fair but I have to learn not to react. I'm 29 and I think I'm going to stay calm now."
A more reflective Grimandi, talking to the Guardian a few weeks later.

FREDDIE LJUNGBERG

"He pissed me off, so I butted him."
Mikael Silvestre, after being sent off for sticking the nut on Ljungberg in 2004/05.

"Could you get us all a pair of those Calvin Klein's? We want the special ones like yours, the ones with a sock down the front. We've seen you in the shower and you're really not that big."
Dennis Bergkamp on Freddie's advert for Calvin Klein.

"(He) can do bugger all for around 75 minutes, have one magic touch and the fans are all falling over themselves to hail him. Or he only has to fart during a warm-up and they're singing his name from the rafters."
Ashley Cole

"He doesn't even talk to me. Why doesn't he talk to me?"
Robin van Persie.

"He was the man who gave me the courage to wear ripped jeans."
Ashley Cole.

"These rumours are completely false. I've only watched two musicals during my entire spell in London and they are Mamma Mia and Saturday Night Fever."
On rumours of homosexuality.

"Amazing player. Very strong, very quick. And the things he did! Certain players have a certain style, a certain movement. With him it looked a little sloppy - with respect I say that - but he did it on purpose."
Dennis Bergkamp.

KANU

"At Arsenal he told me he'd played in nine World Cups - and he was only 23!"
Ray Parlour.

ARSENAL 2 SHEFFIELD UNITED 1
(FA CUP 1999)

"Go on Seaman, you're a gentleman, let one in."
Sheffield United fans in the Clock End.

"I feel robbed, cheated and furious. We were 15 minutes from a replay. We deserve another crack. I could say it should be at Bramall Lane but I don't want to be greedy."
Steve Bruce, United's manager.

"Well that's very decent of him."
A mollified Bruce, after being told Wenger had offered to replay the game.

"We didn't mean to cheat. Kanu did not know. We want to repair what happened. We want it here. We have fair spirit but we are not stupid!"
Arsene Wenger.

"Excuse me while I puke at this sanctimony."
Headline to a piece in the Observer by the infamous Labour spin doctor - and Tottenham fan - Charlie Whelan.

"Would you like to start again?"
Arsenal fans after winning the replay 2-1.

THIERRY HENRY

"I just didn't rate him as a goalscorer and as for overtaking Ian Wright as Arsenal's all-time record goal scorer, not a chance. I was wrong."
Charlie George, admits his first impression was awry.

"I only felt sorry for myself for about a minute."
After missing out on a substitute appearance in the 1998 World Cup final because of Marcel Desailly's sending off.

"The ball came off the beans on toast."
Henry in an interview with Sky Sports, after receiving lessons in rhyming slang from Ray Parlour.

"He was always on about the "dog and bone", too. Thierry was great."
Ray Parlour.

"When we won the league at Tottenham, they came back 2-2 in the last-minute of the game, and they're celebrating – because they're happy to draw against us, obviously. And I remember saying to Mauricio Tarricco, do you realise we only need a point to be Champions? And they all ... So I said 'Yes. Now we're going to celebrate on your pitch. Bye bye!'"

"Negro de mierda".
Description of Henry by Spain coach Luis Aragones, trying to "motivate" Jose Antonio Reyes in November 2004 by telling him 'Say I am better than you, you black shit.'
The subsequent friendly between Spain and England at the Bernebau, was marred by serious racial abuse of England's black players, including Ashley Cole. Reyes was deeply embarrassed by both the incident and the reaction at the game.

"I can see Thierry sat there, focused, in his own world, with his ipod playing on his speakers. Something crap like Michael Jackson would be playing. Then, just before the game he'd belt out a song dedicated to me and to lift the team. '21 seconds' - nothing pumped me up better for a match ... Just thinking about it now brings back the tingle."
Ashley Cole on Henry in My Defence.

"Sometimes you say that God has not given you everything, but with Thierry he has been given a lot."
Arsene Wenger.

"I would love this place to be my garden."
Henry on Highbury.

"An organic machine ... when you are lethal in front of goal and still, after 80 minutes, able to keep up the pace it makes defending very difficult."
Sol Campbell.

"When I kissed the ground after my third, I was saying goodbye to this stadium."
After the final game at Highbury.

"I heard them singing 'Are you watching Arsenal?' Well we were watching. And now we are fourth and this is clear."
Henry, post-Wigan, responding to the fate-temptingly premature (are there any other kind?) chants of Tottenham fans a few weeks earlier.

"It wasn't the fact that we qualified for the CL, it was the fact that we kicked them out and we went in… again!"

"There's Thierry Henry with his wife. Or at least I hope it's his wife."
Gary Lineker, on seeing Henry kissing a woman in the crowd after France's 1-0 win over Brazil in the 2006 World Cup quarter-final.

"I recall meeting him at a club magazine function some time ago and he came up to me and asked if I had seen the game last night. He was talking about Gillingham v Nottingham Forest in the Auto Windscreens Shield."
Andy Exley, editor of the Arsenal magazine.

"I look at Paul Dickov, the way he moves as he's always moving everywhere for another type of game, Kevin Davies, to see what he does, and to annoy players."

"When you put on the shirt of France or Arsenal, you change. It's like a new skin. You become Superman."

"I don't watch cricket. How can you like a game that requires you to take four days off work to follow a Test?"

"And I don't really like golf. I know a lot of English footballers play, but I know that if I go with the club to play, sooner or later I will end up trying to smash the ball with my foot."

"Arsenal is in my blood as well as my heart. I will always, always, always remember you guys. I said I was going to be a Gooner for life and I did not lie because when you are a Gooner, you will always be a Gooner. This club is in my heart and will remain in my heart forever."
None of which stopped him from joining Barcelona.

"I'm not happy because a father that only sees his daughter five times in the last eight months cannot be. If you know what it is to have a daughter then you can imagine what it is like. I'm not asking you to cry for me, only that people don't talk for me."
After joining Barcelona.

"Stop comparing the Henry of Barcelona to the Henry of Arsenal. If you want to see him, buy a Gunners DVD."
Referring to himself in the third person.

"I have said at the time and I will say again that yes I handled the ball. I am not a cheat and never have been. It was an instinctive reaction to a ball that was coming extremely fast in a crowded penalty area."
After the infamous handball goal that knocked Ireland out of a World Cup play-off in the Stade de France.

"I have never denied that the ball was controlled with my hand. I told the Irish players, the referee and the media this after the game. Naturally I feel embarrassed at the way that we won and feel extremely sorry for the Irish who definitely deserve to be in South Africa. There is little more I can do apart from admit that the ball had contact with my hand leading up to our equalising goal and I feel very sorry for the Irish."
On the same incident.

"I am not coming here to be a hero or to prove anything, I am just coming here to help. I'll be on the bench most of the time, if I can make the bench that is. Even if it is just five seconds, one second or just talking in the dressing room, I will give my best, whatever it is."
After rejoining Arsenal on loan in January 2012.

"I don't think I ever felt what I felt when I scored against Leeds," Henry said. "I don't think I'll ever feel that again because that will never come back. I'm not saying I'll never do another comeback.

"I mean you can never have another first goal on a first comeback. That can never be done again. It was kind of weird because everyone was hoping it would happen. You know you dream about something that will never happen? And it did happen. It's weird."
After scoring in his first game back against Leeds.

"Support your team."
Snapping at a fan following a 3-2 defeat at Swansea.

"My friends tell me to embrace it and be happy. And I am. I know about the fun you give to people when you play but for me, the statue is like, a war hero. But I embrace it. What a place to have it. I love Arsenal and to have it right there in front of the stadium. I'm still speechless."
On the unveiling of his statue outside the Emirates.

"We had the opportunity to do it again and I said let's not do this anymore. Let's finish on a high."
Wenger on why he didn't sign Henry for a third time during the 2012-13 season.

ROBERT PIRES

"I would like to introduce you to Robert Pires from Reims. Mark my words, he's going to be a great player."
Robert Sarre of Metz to his chairman Carlo Molinari, after signing Pires from Reims.

"I look forward to him proving it."
Molinari's reply.

"What position are you playing in exactly?"
Marcel Desaiily to Pires after 90 minutes of the Euro 2000 final. Pires responded by setting up Zinedine Zidne's winner.

"I remember what Wenger said to me before the first game, away at Sunderland: "I'm going to leave you on the bench and you're going to see what English football is like." By the 20th minute I was already thinking, what am I doing here?"

"Deceptively fast ... he can accelerate very quickly, despite his slightly flat-footed stance. He always does those little dummies where only his head moves."
Patrick Vieira.

"He speak, me non."
Running away from a television interview after a win at Aston Villa, leaving David Seaman to do the interview on his own.

"Everyone thought I had dived and no-one believed me that the defender had touched me a bit. If he touches me I'm going to fall, as if I was diving into a pool, but he's touched me so it was a penalty."
A not entirely convincing defence of the penalty he earned against Portsmouth during the Invincibles season.

"I knew a player had to go off after that red card but I never thought it would be me. When I saw it was my number, it killed me. I didn't want to kill Wenger, but Jens? Yeah, I'd have killed the German Bastard! It was the worst moment of my career. When I saw the number I thought, no, no, it can't be!"
Pires, four years after the Champions League Final, but by then able to laugh about it.

"11 v 11 it would have been a fantastic game but we had to take Robert Pires off and he still hates me today."
Arsene Wenger.

"I bought the flat only for the memory. For Highbury. I went one day and I cried after, when I saw the development. Only flats now. Strange. I don't like it."
Having bought a flat at the old stadium.

"When I've got a Leo in defence I've always got my gun ready as I know he's going to want to show off at one moment or another and cost us. All parameters have to be considered and I have added one by saying there is astrology involved."
Raymond Domenech explaining his selection criteria and why Pires was left out of the French national team.

"I speak from experience, they were managed by a madman. When I was called up to play for France when he was in charge I felt I was going to a madhouse, I was physically sick. Arsene Wenger used to ask me what was wrong. I would reply that I didn't want to go there, the man is insane."
On Raymond Domenech, after being left out of the French squad for Euro 2008.

"You cannot say it's unintentional. That would be lying and hypocritical."
On Thierry Henry's handball incident v Ireland.

SYLVAIN WILTORD

"Shagga, shagga, shagga!"
After scoring twice in a game Bordeaux won in injury time to take the French title in 1999.

"My game is all about stamina, tenacity, outfoxing your opponent, and when you don't have enough playing time it's difficult to do that on a regular basis. You haven't seen the real Sylvain Wiltord. You see the real me over a season."
To Amy Lawrence of the Guardian during his first season with Arsenal, 2000-01.

"Basically I screwed up."
His own assessment of his performance in the 2001 FA Cup final loss to Liverpool.

"A great striker, a fox in the box. Quiet for a lot of the game and then suddenly popping up from nowhere to be in the right place at the right time to score."
Sol Campbell.

THE 2000 UEFA CUP FINAL

"The Turkish End behind the goal was a frightening site. Packed to the gills with six huge kettle drums hanging over the tunnel. The whole atmosphere from that end was like some ancient army marching to war. The Arsenal fans were as insipid as they have been since Highbury went all seater."
Fan Greg Thomas, on the arseweb website.

"I said to Arsène before the game, 'I'm very worried.' Because there were a few people who weren't at the races because of the Double - a few cracks had started to appear, and it's all about who wants it more, isn't it? But hopefully we've got rid of those people now."
Tony Adams in an interview with Nick Hornby, who believed Adams was referring to Emmanuel Petit and Marc Overmars.

ASHLEY COLE

"He was involved in both and spent so much time on the ground I was wondering when his funeral would be."
Keith Cooper, the UEFA referee assessor, on Cole's alleged role in the red cards for Lee Bowyer and Danny Mills during a volatile 2-1 defeat at home to Leeds in 2001-02.

"I've seen less bad blood between Freddie Mays and Lennie Taylor in one of my favourite films, Gangster No. 1"
Cole, on the 2-0 era-ending defeat at Old Trafford in 2004. Cole nearly had his leg snapped in half by a van Nistlerooy challenge that went unpunished.

"My heart and soul was tied to Arsenal with a fisherman's knot. I don't think even Houdini could have unravelled it. Not for one moment did I see myself leaving."
"The football we'd played was out of this world. No-one was taking more than three touches on the ball: control, turn, pass; control, turn, pass. They couldn't get near us."
On The Invincibles.

"No one could ever call me a prima donna."

"He told me I wasn't earning enough and my salary was going to be increased. My face-cracking smile told him all he needed to know. I was buzzing, really buzzing. His tone soon wiped the smile from my face. I felt his attitude suggested he was doing me a favour, like I was a 17-year-old trainee.
"The deal he offered was a £10,000-a-week increase to £35,000. A hell of a lot of money. But, when taken in the context of football wages and his own estimated value of me of £20 million, and when placed next to those other Arsenal wages of between £80,000 and £100,000 a week, his offer was a piss-take. It was a slap in the face, not a pat on the back."
Cole in his book "My Defence".

"Pini suddenly flicked his wrist to look at his watch. 'Time! Time! My next meeting ...' - and he started to get up out of his chair. The door opened up and Jose Mourinho and Peter Kenyon walked in."
Cole was widely quoted as saying he jumped off his chair in surprise, something he vehemently denied during the enquiry.

"Everyone thought I was lifting up my shirt to kiss the Arsenal badge or wiping away a tear. But it was Patrick and his bloody Vicks."
Cole explains a badge-kissing incident after scoring a goal at Villa after the tapping up scandal. Vieira had grabbed his head in celebration and accidentally rubbed Vicks into Cole's eyes.

"I'm here in the office and David Dein is saying they aren't going to give you £60k a week. They've agreed £55k and this is their best and final offer. Are you happy with that?
When I heard Jonathan repeat the figure of £55k, I nearly swerved off the road. 'He is taking the piss, Jonathan!' I yelled down the phone. I was so incensed. I was trembling with anger."
Cole in "My Defence" again, arguably the greatest PR own goal ever scored by a footballer, in a field where the competition is fierce.

"Why not do it in the middle of the M25 and then at least everybody knows?"
Wenger on the meeting.

"To the right side of my car, on the pavement were a gang of Arsenal fans who had been stood outside a pub, and they were on the kerb yelling at me; their faces twisted with hate. Stupidly I thought I could reason with them. I wound down my window.
'You fuck off to Chelsea, you traitor,' yelled one of them."

"I love this place. But I can't do this no more."
Cole to Thierry Henry after the final game at Highbury. Cole was hoping the fans would sing his name, but he was ignored - and had to be consoled by the captain.

"I've got too much pride for this shit babes, people are going to think I want to join Chelsea!"
Ashley to his wife Cheryl.

"Babe, you are never going to believe where Jordan is getting married today."
Cole breaks the devastating news to Cheryl. Jordan and Peter Andre have got married at Highclere Castle, where the Coles had been intending to wed.

"Before the game there was all this stuff about anti-racism and anti-bullying. It would be a good idea to start wearing wristbands for anti-diving."
Roy Keane on an alleged dive by Cole during Arsenal's 4-2 loss to Manchester United at Highbury in 2004-05.

"He is quiet, shy and surprisingly reserved."
Cole's agent, Jonathan Barnett.

"In the new era (2005-06) too many people took constructive criticism way too personally. So I learned to say nothing to keep the peace in the dressing room."

"I stood looking up at the fans in the tiers, taking it all in, looking at that mass of red and white and thinking, 'I'll always be an Arsenal fan, even if I'm not an Arsenal player'."
After the 2006 Champions League final defeat.

"For me the love weren't there no more."

"It's hard Ashley. It's like a divorce I suppose."
Wenger to Cole, on hearing the latter wanted to leave.

"GAY AS YOU GO." "SO WHO BUMIT?"
Headlines in the News of the World and the Sun. Cole was subjected to an orchestrated campaign of innuendo in the tabloid press, implying he'd been filmed engaging in homosexual sex acts. Cole sued and the papers withdrew the allegations.

Arsenal fans get it, I left I won #ihaveastaronmyshirtnow'
On twitter after winning the Champions League with Chelsea.

FRANCIS JEFFERS

"Maybe people will be surprised that I have signed an Englishman but I looked at his quality and not his passport. Francis is a 'fox in the box'."
Arsene Wenger, after signing Jeffers in 2001.

"We were considering Ruud van Nistlerooy and Francis Jeffers and in the end end we went for Jeffers."

"The red card was deserved. Francis knows he overreacted and should not have done it. He's apologised. He realised he made a mistake. He's intelligent, he's young and he'll learn."
Wenger after Jeffers was sent off in the 2003 Charity Shield v Manchester United, shortly before loaning him to Everton.

"I've still had a good career and I still believe I've been blessed. I'm confident that I've got another four years in me if I can find another club and start banging the goals in."
After signing for Floriana of Malta in October 2012.

SOL CAMPBELL

"Cheer up Sulzeer, you're two-one up!"
An unnamed West Ham coach to Campbell during a very brief spell with West Ham. Campbell asked what the coach meant. When he realised "you" meant a reference to the West Indies cricket team, who were beating England 2-1, he felt the remark was racist, walked out of the Boleyn Ground and only returned years later as a Tottenham player.

"When I played for Arsenal it was not far from what Tottenham were trying to achieve. Only we had the players."

"Every time he speaks to me I have this image of him showing me his pips on his uniform."
Campbell on George Graham.

"I was on £13,500 per week... I had muppets as team mates who were on treble the money."
On the wage structure at Spurs.

"Let's hope this speech isn't too long."
Campbell's thought ahead of his first ever one-to-one meeting with new Spurs manager Christian Gross.

"I'm not going anywhere"
Campbell in November 2000. This was taken by Spurs fans as an indication that he was staying at White Hart Lane. It could also be read as an accurate summing-up of the state of his career in N17 at that point.

"There is no chance of Sol leaving for Arsenal. He is a Spurs fan and there is not a hope in hell of him playing in an Arsenal shirt."
David Buchler, Tottenham's vice-chairman. In May 2001.

"I always dreamed of winning the league at White Hart Lane. So I left and joined Arsenal."

"Boss, if you tell Sol to sit at the front of the bus, then we'll all sit towards the back and we won't all get hit."
Unnamed senior player to Arsene Wenger before Sol's first return to White Hart Lane as an Arsenal player in 2001-02, quoted by the Mirror's John Cross. 4000 balloons with the word "Judas" were released by Spurs fans at the game.

"We hate you because we loved you."
Banner unfurled at White Hart Lane before Campbell's first game for Arsenal at Tottenham. The wording is exactly the same as that used by Barcelona fans when Luis Figo played his first game for Real Madrid at the Camp Nou, though they went a step further by throwing a pig's head at Figo.

"When I saw them carrying signs with Judas on them I thought oh hell, this will be a real test for Sol."
Wenger on the reception Campbell received from Tottenham's fans on his first return to White Hart Lane as an Arsenal player.

"I was looking at the faces in the Spurs end. Then I caught sight of him. A knife to my heart. Behind the goal, I knew that face. My older brother, Tony, a Spurs fan, in among the slurry of bile violating my name."
Campbell, stunned to see his elder brother form part of the mob during the same game. The pair have rarely spoken since.

"We've got Campbell, we've got Campbell, we've got Campbell, from the Lane.
"You've got Vega, you've got Vega, You've got Vega, from the Lane."
Sung by Arsenal fans during an FA Cup 3rd round tie at Watford in 2001-02.

"I was really fucked off that we gave away that last-minute goal... to see Jens throw it away like that really pissed me off. So there's everyone enjoying themselves and I'm having a right go at Jens."
After the 2-2 draw with Spurs that secured the 2003-04 title.

"It had a psychological impact on us but again because of the way we were defeated. That was far more upsetting, losing like that, because they just seem to get away with it. You try and tell yourself that these things balance out over the course of a season, but I've had so many rough decisions against them you begin to wonder . . ."
Campbell on the Old Trafford defeat in 2004-05, in an interview with the Guardian's Donald McCrae.

"It was a terrible decision. He dived, as simple as that. He knew, I knew and by the end of the game everyone watching on television also knew. I refused to shake his hand at the end. He cheated."
On Rooney's dive in the same match.

"He had his boots off and I said come on Sol, put those on and let's get on with the game. I remember he shook his head and said 'I can't.' I knew then something was very wrong. 'Can't' isn't something Sol Campbell says.
Thierry Henry, after Campbell vanished from Highbury at half-time during a home defeat to West Ham in the 2005-06 season.

"It is a big surprise to me because he cancelled his contract to go abroad. Have you sold Portsmouth to a foreign country?"
Wenger on Sol Campbell.

"I'm 30 now and in five years' time I won't be in this country. That's definite. Italy looks good to me because it would suit my kind of football. Spain is an option."
Before joining Portsmouth, Notts County, Arsenal (again) and finally Newcastle.

"Sol, Sol, wherever you maybe, you're on the brink of lunacy. And we don't care if you're swinging from a tree, you Judas cunt with HIV."
Tottenham song, sang to the tune of Lord of the Dance. As the Guardian's Simon Hattenstone pointed out: "To its credit, it is a brilliantly tight verse, addressing any number of prejudices in four little lines. There's something to offend everybody here - the mentally ill, HIV sufferers, gay people, women, with an allusion to racist lynching thrown in for good measure."
Some Tottenham fans were appalled by this song, but it was still sung by thousands at Fratton Park in 2008 when Campbell was playing for Portsmouth.

"It's out of hand now. This is a human rights situation. If this happened on the street you would be arrested."
Campbell after the Portsmouth v Spurs game.

"That is just not acceptable. You have to get the ringleaders. People follow the main men like sheep, and if you get the main culprits you've got a chance of dealing with it."
Tony Adams, welcoming the news that arrests had been made.

"I felt absolutely disgusted at this and I didn't react because of my profile and I feared I might make the situation worse and cause problems.
I felt totally victimised and helpless by the abuse I received on this day. It has had an effect on me personally and I do not want it to continue. I support the police in their action."
Campbell after a court found two Spurs fans guilty of homophobic abuse and banned them from attending matches for three years.

"You surprised me last season Sol. I never knew you had it in you."
Arsene Wenger to Campbell after he rejoined Arsenal for six months during the Januray 2010 transfer window.
Campbell being Campbell, he took the remark as hurtful when Wenger had meant it as a compliment.

GIOVANNI VAN BRONCKHORST

"We nearly didn't sign him because the letters did not fit on his shirt."
David Dein.

"The Horse feeds the Horst."
Commentator Jonathan Pearce after Oleg "The Horse" Luzhny, set up a van Bronckhorst goal.

KOLO TOURE

"We were doing a one-v-one drill in training and I was so hungry to make an impression. I slid into a tackle near the side of the pitch and Arsene Wenger was just on the touchline. As I slid in, I tackled him too and he ended up on the floor."
Toure on his trial with Arsenal. Wenger picked himself up and said: "I will sign this player."

Four weeks before, I was watching you all on TV in the Ivory Coast and then I was training with you. Those players had an incredible mentality."
To Martin Keown in a Daily Mail interview in 2014.

"I came from Arsenal, where everything was so straightforward. The manager was so calm. Mark Hughes was the same, he was great. But Mancini was different. Balotelli was not a problem for me. You just had to know how to handle him and I knew how to get along with him. He kept asking me, 'Why aren't you playing, Kolo?' I said, 'Ask your father, Mancini'."
On life at Man City.

PASCAL CYGAN

"The difference between France and England in terms of the physical game is that in France only the defenders kick you, pull your shirt or are tricky. In England it is the whole of the team who do that."
Coming to terms with English football, in an interview with Henry Winter of the Telegraph.

"He's bald, he's shit, he plays when no one's fit."
Song reflecting Cygan's popularity.

"Pascal Cygan needs another 183 goals to break Ian Wright's scoring record."
Stadium announcer at Highbury after Cygan scored twice against Fulham, at a time when Thierry Henry was closing in on Wright's landmark.

"I have only great memories of that era. You know when you're playing with players like Vieira, Henry, Bergkamp, Kanu, Pires and Wiltord you can only have good memories. I learned and enormous amount. I was playing with the best players on the planet and I think for that reason alone people must envy me."

JENS LEHMANN

"My coach confirmed to me my impression that he uses a different measuring stick to evaluate Almunia. For me, this was a huge disappointment. That has forced me to think about my situation. I have to ask myself what is still realistic and possible for me at Arsenal? When Wenger says something like that, it's going to be difficult for me to get back in here. It's very frustrating. When I see the performances on the field, I get angry and I have to clench my fist in my pocket."
After being dropped in the 2004/05 season.

"If I have a lot of adrenaline in my body, that is helpful because I feel less pain."

"At the moment I'm just swallowing it all as part of the humiliation but I think – and this is aimed at my dear manager – one shouldn't humiliate players for too long."

"It was the hardest decision of his coaching career so I accepted that I should be No 1 and that was it."
Having been chosen ahead of Oliver Kahn for the 2006 World Cup by German manager Jurgen Klinnsmann.

"I do not have a 24-year-old girlfriend. I have another life altogether."
On Oliver Kahn's choice of partner.

"I am without a doubt mentally the strongest player at Arsenal because I have more experience. There will always be a keeper who will play better for two or three matches but I have never seen anyone do this for ten games. I know that I have an advantage at Arsenal and that I can keep it. I don't see any young supermen keeping me out. I know I will be playing again at Arsenal. The coach will let me play. He knows it, and I know it – it doesn't matter if I have another week out. I have read that Almunia said he deserves to be the No 1 but until now he has not won a single important game."

"He didn't hate me, but Jens is the kind of person who, when someone tries to take his place, he fights and fights and fights to recover it. He's very competitive and I just got in the way.
"In his last season at Arsenal there was a team dinner for us all to say goodbye. Jens and me didn't speak — and I mean never — but he came to me with his wife and showed me a totally different face. I thought, 'Oh my God, who is this? This is not Jens!' We talked about life, football, Spain, Germany, everything."
Manuel Almunia.

"Wojciech is a good goalkeeper too, but he needs to be more mature. Not on the pitch, where he's good, but he needs to be more quiet and settled off the pitch. He should think twice before doing certain things. When you're young you do things without thinking."
Advice for his successor Wojciech Szcesny.

"Jens, why can't you be normal?"
Stuttgart fan to Lehmann in the week he'd criticised the board, urinated on an advertising hoarding during a match, conceded a penalty and been sent off against Mainz.
Lehmann responded by stealing the fans glasses and walking off with them, only giving them back after a 10-minute pursuit.

"Sometimes you've just got to go."
Lehmann explaining the first incident.

"It reminds me a lot of the Tour de France - sometimes you don't have any other possibility but to let it out."
His sporting director Horst Heldt, explaining why Lehmann hadn't been sacked.

"Anyone doing that would be nuts. You can't foresee what would happen. You can't advise anyone to do so - they would no longer have fun playing football... Football is a man thing. You shower together every day."
After his former Germany team mate Thomas Hitzlsperger came out as a homosexual.

JOSE ANTONIO REYES

"We didn't think he would play on Sunday because he was suspended – that makes me think he has all the qualities to join Arsenal."
Wenger, after signing Reyes from Seville.

"It's like you wanting to marry Miss World and she doesn't want you. I can try to help you but if she does not want to marry you what can I do?"
Arsene Wenger on Reyes' desire to join Real Madrid.

"Despite the global warming, England is still not warm enough for him."
Wenger again.

CESC FABREGAS

"With all due respect to Cesc, he's no Patrick. It's like putting the gloves of a heavyweight champion on the hands of an unproven featherweight and telling him to go out there and knock out the opposition."
Ashley Cole.

"It was a dream of mine to play for Barca, but I was not bitter at Arsenal. On the contrary, I was living somewhere which, for me, was the most beautiful city in the world, I was in an incredible team with a superb coach and supporters I adored. It was not a question of life or death. If Barca had not come in for me, I would have played my whole career at Arsenal. That was certain."
On his departure.

"Arsenal is in my heart and always will be. It was important for me to leave the right way. I think the fans understood. I don't know if I'll have the opportunity to go back and play there one day, or maybe after football. The club's like a family so even if it wasn't as a coach, I'm sure they'd give me the chance to play a role. It's a club that is always going to be there and will always open its doors to me."
Fabregas to Sid Lowe of the Guardian in October 2013.

"Yes everyone knows that Arsenal had the first option to sign me. They decided not to take this option and therefore it wasn't meant to be. I wish them well in the future."
Quote from Fabregas after signing for Chelsea which was edited out of Chelsea's subsequent media release.

"Snake."
Remark made by an Arsenal supporting Chelsea steward to Fabregas during the 2015-16 season. The steward was subsequently sacked.

GAEL CLICHY

"I had a seven-hour operation to sew everything back on but at some point I had a problem with my lungs and my heart stopped for 30 seconds."
Clichy narrowly avoided death as a 15-year-old after complications following an accident when he climbed a fence and ripped the end of a finger off.

"I really believe if you are a player who thinks only about money you could end up at Manchester City."
A few months before signing for Manchester City.

"I am leaving Arsenal within the next two weeks. Thank you for all your support and great memories. You all will always be in my heart."
A few days before signing for Manchester City.

PHILLIPPE SENDEROS

"He's a lucky player. I've been watching him, he keeps making mistakes. His real luck is that none of his mistakes have been taken advantage of. But it won't last."
Sol Campbell, after losing his place to Senderos in the 2004-05 season, from his autobiography.

MATHIEU FLAMINI

"He's intelligent and he knows the system. He's more calculating than you would think."
Jose Anigo, Flamini's manager at Olympique Marseilles after the player engineered a move to Arsenal, showing a better knowledge of contractual law than his club.

"Beautiful treason."
Anigo on Flamini's departure.

"Arsenal are in my heart and they will be in my heart for ever. I will always be an Arsenal fan and leaving was not easy."
A year after signing for AC Milan.

"In the Premier League you see tackles like that every week. Of course, it is always important to play the ball. But I went for the ball. In four years in England I don't think I was ever sent off straight away. It's not like I have a reputation for bad tackles. Most of the time at Arsenal we were the team that was kicked."
After a "horror" tackle on Vedran Corluka while playing for Milan against Tottenham.

"I do not like that and he will not do that again. I was surprised he did that; we don't want that."
Arsene Wenger after Flamini cut the sleeves off his long-sleeved shirt, violating Arsenal's policy that every player should wear the same length of sleeve.

"I've been playing at the top level for 10 years, I like to wear short sleeves, that's what I like to do."
Flamini explaining himself.

"Do it again and I will make you blind."
Remark Flamini was alleged to have made to Stoke's Marc Wilson after a foul on Jack Wilshere.

MAN UTD 2 ARSENAL 0 2004

"Old Trafford is an amazing place to play when it is a full house but it has never intimidated me. I'm not sure I could say the same for Mike Riley."
Ashley Cole after having his leg gashed by van Nistlerooy. Cole was incredulous when told Sky Sports hadn't even replayed the incident. Van Nistlerooy was retrospectively banned for three-games.

"My thought process was simple: 'He's a great player, a pacey, tricky winger. If I stand off him and don't tackle, he'll run rings round me and make me look an idiot. He's got more skill, he's got more speed. I might have more stamina but that's not going to be much good if he's ripped me apart in the first 30 minutes."
Gary Neville on Jose Antonio Reyes, in his autobiography.

"Some say I crossed the line. How? Reyes was subbed after 70 minutes and it wasn't for his own protection. He didn't have a mark on his leg. Yes, there was a time in the first half when he knocked the ball through my legs and, chasing back, I went through him and tripped him. It wasn't pretty but it's something any defender does dozens of times a season: you concede a foul high up the pitch rather than risk worse trouble around the penalty area."
Neville again.

"Ferguson's out of order. He has lost all sense of reality. He is going out looking for a confrontation, then asking the person he is confronting to apologise. He's pushed the cork in a bit far this time."
Arsene Wenger.

"This slice of pizza came flying over my head and hit Fergie straight in the mush ... We all went back in the dressing room and fell about laughing ... the United boys did their best not to laugh."
Ashley Cole.

"I've got a fair idea who launched it and his aim with a pizza is just as good as his skills with a ball, but I'm no grass and won't name names. All I'll say is the culprit wasn't English or French, so that should narrow it down."
Cole again.

"Don't worry, the manager knows it wasn't you."
Rio Ferdinand to Ashley Cole. (Slightly sinister?)

MANUEL ALMUNIA

"To be sitting on the bench behind somebody who only started to play when he was 30 is not funny."
Jens Lehmann.

"He does not have my class."
Jens again.

"I went from being No 1 to No 3 almost overnight, but I tried not to think about it. Maybe I should have left one year earlier, but I had a contract that was too good to refuse."
On why he stayed at Arsenal.

ROBIN VAN PERSIE

"I am the Thierry now, I am their god and I will do wassup because I am the king."
Theo Walcott's toe-curling account of RVP's re-enactment of Henry's 'wassup' celebration, from his autobiography.

"I've received many proposals to leave Arsenal, but my heart speaks louder and will not let me leave."

"I don't have the inclination to go anywhere. I want to win trophies with Arsenal, not anyone else. I know you can win trophies in many countries and in many ways, but I want to do that in our way."

"The boss told us to put up with his 'little ways' because he scored lots of goals for us, but at times it was so hard."
Walcott again.

"I have kept quiet all this time out of respect and loyalty for the club and as agreed with Mr. Gazidis and Mr. Wenger, but since there is so much speculation in the media, I think it is fair for you guys to know what's really going on at the moment."
Robin's way of bracing "you guys" for the bad news.

"Out of my huge respect for Mr. Wenger, the players and the fans I don't want to go into any details, but unfortunately in this meeting it has again become clear to me that we in many aspects disagree on the way Arsenal FC should move forward."
Robin, perhaps confusing the role of "captain" and "Chief Executive".

"I love the club and the fans, no matter what happens. I have grown up and became a man during my time with Arsenal FC."

THE 2005 FA CUP FINAL

"We knew we had to be a little bit more cautious than usual because we knew we had less attacking potential than we normally have."
Arsene Wenger, referring to Thierry Henry's absence.

"They were trying to hammer me and get on my back and I just wanted to shove it down their mouths."
Ashley Cole, on the abuse he received from Man Utd fans.

"You have to give credit to Manchester United. They created so many chances. We worked very hard for each other, maybe some will say we did not deserve to win but our spirit was fantastic. We took it right to the end but had no real power to go forward."
Patrick Vieira.

"Patrick seems to have an immunity to these kind of things so I'm not surprised."
Alex Ferguson, claiming Vieira should have been sent off.

ABOU DIABY

"We have always kept the younger players which our coach wanted to use. But Diaby did not play so this was a strategic sale for us."
Auxerre's vice-president Gerard Borgoin, after selling Diaby to Arsenal for £2 million in the January 2006 transfer window.

"Abou was one of the players I used at the start of the season and then he had to stop because of repetitive injuries. Maybe he was attracted by England and the money there. This probably did not force him to make all the necessary efforts to come back to his best level with us."
Auxerre's then manager Jacques Santini.

"The only thing they've got in common is that they're both tall and they're both brothers."
Ian Wright on comparisons of Diaby with Vieira.

"I accept that I do need to be more aggressive and more physical. I can tackle, I think I can anyway. I think I have the ability to have more of an impact in the middle, I am not lazy. People think I am because of the way I run, that I am not working as hard as I can, but trust me I am."

"Made of paper."
Ray Parlour, after yet another Diaby injury.

"Abou, do you have a Spurs shirt?"
"Yes Younes, he gave me one."
"Do you wear it in the street?"
"No, at home. In the street I'd be attacked!"
Diaby in a joint interview with his boyhood friend, Tottenham's Younes Kaboul which was unsurprisingly taken out of context by the British tabloids.

"I've never given up hope of going to the World Cup. Thinking of that has kept me going. Once I'm back on pitch, everything's possible." Nine out of ten players would've given up. People who say Diaby is fragile are wrong. He is Highlander."
Talking to France Football in March 2014.

THEO WALCOTT

"Can run through puddles and not make a splash."
Harry Redknapp.

"Walcott had no right to be there."
Steven Gerrard on Walcott's inclusion in the 2006 World Cup squad.

"He's the most grounded young man I've ever met at the top level of sport. He's a credit to his mum and dad."
Bob Wilson, asked by 4-4-2 to choose his fantasy nephew.

EMMANUEL ADEBAYOR

"If I was Argentinian or Brazilian, people would consider me differently. I feel the young and little Togolese is not looked at with the same eyes. I can't go on like that, I have to leave. It is not a sporting matter as the players and technical staff have always supported me."
Early signs of unhappiness at Monaco.

"I never told anyone I would be leaving this club, never ever. I'm very happy we've found a solution."
After deciding to spurn Milan and Barcelona and sign a new deal, August 2008.

"I am a footballer, I have a three-year contract at Arsenal but as you know, a lot of clubs are interested in me... At the moment we are just going to sit down and talk and decide what to do. Nothing has been decided yet. We will decide next week."
In an interview with Sky Sports, less than an hour after "clearing up" his future with the previous quote.

"Arsenal put me where I am today. They made me one of the biggest strikers in the world. I have to pay them back. How am I going to pay them back? Make them win trophies. That's what I am here for and I have to fight for that. Next season, 100 per cent, I am an Arsenal footballer."
May 2009 and Adebayor tells Arsenal's website he's staying again.

"I was born to play football and that is what I want to do. I have come here to make history for this club and those supporters. It's what the chairman and the manager told me that they want too and I can't wait to get started."
On joining Man City a couple of months later for a reported salary that trebled his Arsenal wages.

"Under it (his tattoo) you can see I put 'Only God can judge me'. And what I can see today in today's world is most of the people and a lot of people are trying to judge people,

which is not correct. So you are not my creator, you are not the one, you are not the people who create me, so they have to leave the choice to the Almighty God to judge me."
"If 100 people see it 99 will say it's bad and the 100th will be Mark Hughes."
Wenger, after Adebayor allegedly stamped on Van Persie's head during a 4-2 win for Manchester City over Arsenal in 2009-10.

"In football, everybody is free to have an opinion. If somebody stamps on your head in that way, you wouldn't say, 'thank-you very much' and turn the other cheek. Only Jesus Christ did that. You know exactly at that fraction, I can injure somebody or I cannot injure somebody and you ease off or you leave in. In England, you have many cases where the players leave in, less now than 10 years ago. I have seen some challenges where if you do that in the street, you go to jail."
On the same challenge and broadening the debate.

"He has shown a real lack of class today, to me and the fans."
RVP's take on Adebayor after the same match.

"I have weighed up my feelings in the weeks and months since the attack and I am still haunted by the events which I witnessed on that horrible afternoon on the Togo team bus. We were just footballers going to play a football match and represent our country, yet we were attacked by people who wanted to kill us all. It is a moment I will never forget and one I never want to experience again."
Retiring from international football after the terrorist attack on the Togo team bus at the 2010 Africa Cup of Nations.

"It should have been you."
The indefensible response sung by some of Arsenal's fans in the ensuing North London derby at White Hart Lane.

THE 2006 CHAMPIONS LEAGUE FINAL

"The moment he blew he knew he'd done wrong. I looked at him and saw him cursing himself 'sheeeeet!' ... the ref buckled and sent Jens off, egged on by the Barcelona players who surrounded him, sticking their hands in the air, screaming red card, red card."
Ashley Cole, a player who knew a thing or two about lobbying for red cards, trying to impersonate Norwegian referee Terje Hauge's accent.

"No one picked me up. Barcelona seemed arrogant, like he won't be any trouble or whatever. Once it left my head I knew it was a goal."
Sol Campbell.

"We'd probably have chosen 1-0 down with 11 men still on the pitch than 0-0 with ten men and Jens and Pires off the pitch."
Cole.

"We didn't lose to Barcelona, we lost to the ref."
Henry.

WILLIAM GALLAS

"You're nothing but a little cunt. If you can't control the ball go back to Guadeloupe. Do you think your parents left you here for you to fail?"
A motivational speech to Gallas by his coach at Clairefontaine, Francisco Filho.

"Find a true left back or right back, but not me."
To Olympique Marseilles manager Javier Clemente.

"This game will always leave a bitter taste ... I had to play in three different positions! At the start of the game we were 1-0 up and succeeded in blocking Thierry Henry as well as we could, so I don't understand why they bombed me out to left-back. At that moment we let in a goal. 1-1. 20 minutes later they told me : 'William, change, you're playing right back'. It was madness, I didn't understand anything anymore. At the end we'd lost 3-1, when we'd been comfortably 1-0 up."
Gallas on the 2002 FA Cup final, when he played for Chelsea against Arsenal. His memory failed him, Chelsea never led and Arsenal won 2-0.

"When Jose Mourinho generously offered him a way back into the 'family' after the American tour, this was thrown back in the Chelsea manager's face. The manager told him that, even if he did not agree a new contract but returned to the 'family' and abided by the rules, he would still select the best players available and would not punish him playing wise. He threatened that if he was forced to play, or if he was disciplined and financially punished for his breach of the rules, he could score an own goal or get himself sent off, or make deliberate mistakes. However, despite meetings to try and resolve the problems Gallas made it clear to Jose Mourinho he would never play for Chelsea again."
Official press release from Chelsea FC, prior to Gallas's swap deal with Ashley Cole.

"All this is very, very petty on behalf of Chelsea, but at the same time, coming on behalf of its new leaders, that does not surprise me. Even if Chelsea has much money, its new leaders lack class."
Gallas's response.

"Our players were too young to handle the pressure. The average age was around 24, which meant we had kids of 20 or 22 years old and I sensed they would have trouble staying on the road. I'd been there and I knew what goes on in the head."
Gallas on the incident that left Eduardo with a broken leg at Birmingham in February 2008.

"Gallas is in a state of disbelief."
BBC commentator Jonathan Pearce as Gallas showed the youngsters how to handle such pressure by storming off the pitch, throwing a tantrum that meant he had to be restrained by an official. He then sat on the pitch and started crying.

"I'll never make a mistake like that again. Was it a good attitude for a player? No. Was it a good reaction from a captain? No. (But) it makes me think of Zinedine Zidane and I understand his reaction to Materazzi at the World Cup final."
A grudging admission of regret in his autobiography.

"He starts crying after the final whistle. I played for managers who would be turning in their graves."
Alan Hansen.

"I know my strengths, I know my qualities and I know what I am worth."

"Who do you think you are? You're only 20 years old. You're not my friend."
Gallas to Nasri on the bus at Euro 2008, after Nasri had refused to give up his seat on the bus to Thierry Henry.

"When the moment came I had a choice. Either I could say nothing and then during training I could take him down a peg by giving him a kick on the ankle, or I could tell him his fortune."
Gallas responds to Nasri's Rosa Parks moment and elects to take the latter option.

"When, as captain, some players come up to you and talk to you about a player complaining about him and then during the match you speak to this player and the player in question insults us, there comes a time where we can no longer comprehend how this can happen. I am trying to defend myself a bit without giving names. Otherwise I'm taking it all (the blame). It's very frustrating. I'm 31, the player is six years younger than me."
Gallas generously decides not to name names after a furious dressing row following a 4-4 draw with Tottenham at the Emirates, an outburst that cost him his job as captain.

BACARY SAGNA
"Arsene Wenger is a major reason why I signed for Arsenal. He is an excellent manager with a fantastic record and I am really looking forward to working with him."
After joining from Auxerre in 2007.

"I disconnected. It was a childhood fear, losing someone close to me. As a result I tried to avoid the subject. Not just forget about his death but go back to my life as it was beforehand, when he was there."
After the death of his brother Omar, in 2008.

"When a winger went by me I didn't give a fuck. As far as football was concerned I lost my concentration and tenacity. During matches I sometimes felt I was seeing things in slow-motion. I'd become someone who couldn't give a fuck and after training I'd return home and would be unable to remember the journey. Things had lost their taste."
On his struggle to cope.

"It's as if they are upset that some of us left the country which is quite crazy. They have made us out to be silly boys who wanted to leave early and that's bad.
"When I left they said I would be on the bench, that I wouldn't be in Arsenal's team. But what should I have done? I was playing for Auxerre and then Arsenal, one of the biggest teams in Europe, called me, but I am still expected to stay in France!"
On the French media.

"On the pitch there is a war, but off the pitch we are all friends, I'm not angry at him because he signed for our rivals."

Sagna on Gallas before the latter returned to the Emirates with Tottenham. A subsequent headline was "Sagna Declares War On Gallas".

I keep reading I left for money, I'm greedy, whatever. All I want to say is I stayed in Arsenal with the same contract since 2008. I never asked for money, so people who think that it's for money, it's not."

"Arsenal made me grow up as a player and as a man. I believe Arsenal have a great team. Arsenal have a lot of quality. I just personally wanted a boost, like I said – start from the bottom and try to find my space."

"We want you to stay."
Song from the crowd, directed at Sagna after the 2014 FA Cup Final. He smiled. And subsequently joined Manchester City.

NICKLAS BENDTNER

"I want to be top scorer in the Premier League, top scorer at the World Cup and within five years I want to be among the best strikers in the world. Trust me, it will happen."
After being named Denmark's player of the year for 2009.

"I love my pink boots. I've wanted to play in that colour ever since I was young."

"I've never seen anyone else playing in pink boots before. I think it's an outstanding colour and looks amazing. But I don't think anyone at Arsenal is going to be able to compete with me on that front. I have reached the top of the outstanding boots. The only way they can beat me now is to play in diamond-encrusted boots. And I don't think that's going to happen for a few years."

"There is a price to pay as well for us players. The biggest thing I miss because of football is that I really, really love to go on a skiing holiday but as long as I have my career, I can't do that because of the risk of being injured."
On his alleged £52,000 per week wages.

"It is wrong to compare my salary to the salary of businessmen. Compare it movie actors instead."

"I love the fact we share the same style and I hope I can be as successful as him."
Nicky on Robert Pires.

"I should start every game, I should be playing every minute of every match and always be in the team."

"The way a footballer shows off what he wears says a great deal about his personality."

"If you ask me if I am one of the best strikers in the world, I say yes because I believe it. I reimbursed supporters who had bought shirts with my 26 number because it was early in the season when I made the change. But it was only after I asked Eduardo for the No 9 and he said no that I decided to do something different."

Nicky after changing his shirt number to 52 - it was rumoured because this was the amount in thousands he earned a week.

"My body is my livelihood and I was desperate to find out if I was ok. So I took off all my clothes, even my pants, picked up a wing mirror that had come off the car and checked myself over, front and back."
After crashing his £160,000 car on a sliproad to the M25 off the A1. Nicky said he was taking evasive action.

LASSANA DIARRA
"I feel like I never played at Arsenal. If people don't remind me of that fact I just forget it. It has been wiped from my mind."

SAMIR NASRI
"I don't think you can blame that on the fact that I sat in Thierry Henry's seat."
Responding to William Gallas's claim that he shouldn't have sat in a senior player's place during Euro 2008.

"Despite letting us down with his move to Manchester I always liked Samir and am genuinely sorry to think of him all the way up there as the 'forgotten man' of City."
Theo Walcott wafts his claws at Nasri in his surprisingly revealing autobiography.

"Someone had tipped Ray (Parlour) the wink about Nasri's chin paranoia. He walked over to Samir, tapping his neck and going "blimey mate, you look like you've already won THE DOUBLE,' pointing at his chin. Samir was fuming, it was 'merde' this and 'putain' that for the rest of the day."
Walcott again.

"An old school friend of mine worked at Grosvenor House, on Park Lane, and he said that Samir and entourage were always noisy, in the bar and the restaurant and their rooms and they would shout at the female staff, and leer at them, and spit on the carpets. The last straw was when he mistook the bidet in his room for the toilet."
Walcott, prepares for the knock out blow.

"When he left it really left a bitter taste in our mouths as we had all asked him to his face if he was staying or going and he had always maintained that he was staying at Arsenal. I hear from friends up there that he quickly began to regret his decision, but unfortunately that's football."
Walcott, leaving Nasri on the canvas.

"Roberto signed me and I started games but he would take me off before the end. We had some disagreements and I had some problems with him, as his methods are very different to Arsene Wenger's at Arsenal. He would arrive at the training ground and not even say hello. He'd just tell you what he wanted to do. Wenger would go round the dressing room every day and talk with his players. You could express yourself."
Nasri in The Sun, after Mancini was sacked by City, backing up Walcott's claim.

"I know that training every day I will improve, there is a lot of intensity. It's the level above Arsenal, when we finish the session with a game it feels like a competition game. I chose a club on the way up."
To France Football magazine.

"Shut the fuck up!"
Nasri to the French media, immediately after his equaliser in France's 1-1 draw with England during Euro 2012, accompanied with a shush gesture.

"Can I have a quote Samir?"
"You're always looking to write shit."
"In that case you can get lost."
"Fuck you, go fuck your mother you son of a bitch. There, now you can say that I was brought up badly."
Nasri to a journalist from AFP after France's Euro 2012 quarter-final defeat to Spain.

"The supporters and in particular children should know that I regret that my language may have shocked them."
Nasri's subsequent apology.

ALEX SONG

"When I arrived at Arsenal I didn't know anyone, could not speak a word of English and hated the food. My first two years here were very difficult. I would cry alone in my hotel room. When I finished training I would spend all my time on the phone with my friends in France. I ran up a huge phone bill."

"I am at the right club. Forget Barcelona, Arsenal is the best club. Arsenal have given me everything and I love this place. If I had to leave I would break down and cry. It's still my dream to win the league here."
Before joining Barcelona.

ANDRE ARSHAVIN

"I am Gooner."
Arshavin, after signing for Arsenal in the January 2009 transfer window.

"I think I'd be lying if I called myself a patriot of the club."

Q: Andrey, what do you think people need pain for?
Arshavin: For people not to forget that they are mere mortals. Some people say that suffering purifies the soul.

From RinaBeer
Q: Hi. I am 25 years old and I'm still not married. My parents are very upset about this. They say I can end up a spinster. But I don't want to get married yet. What shall I do? (Sorry if this is off topic; just
 want to know your opinion)
 Arshavin: I think I can help you.

Step 1: You need to find a scruffy heavy drinker.
Step 2: Once you've found him, try to persuade him to "marry" you. I think that for a small amount of money, he will agree to fulfill the role of your fiance? :)
Final: Bring this guy home. Tell your parents he'll live with you ;)
I think next time they will think better before forcing their opinion on you.
Highlights from a surreal "Ask Andre" Q and A on his official website, from April 2010.

"The atmosphere was weird. It felt like the crowd was at the theatre — good seats, expensive tickets and they wanted to see a show, not to support the team.

"It was like there was no advantage in playing at home. Many of the players — the leaders that were left from the club's time at Highbury — often complained that the atmosphere in the stands was so bad."
Andre, quoted in The Sun.

LAURENT KOSCIELNY

"I do think about it sometimes. Mistakes can happen in life. It was hard for the fans and for the club, but life goes on, there are things more important than losing a final. There will be plenty more finals to play and win. It was tough to swallow but it made me a better player and a better person."
To the Arsenal website, a few months after the defeat to Birmingham in the 2011 League Cup Final.

PER MERTESACKER

"He doesn't look very mobile – he looks a bit slow. Obviously, he's played a lot for Germany, but if he really is top-class, why has no-one else come in for him. Even Bayern Munich haven't."
Peter Storey.

OLIVIER GIROUD

"The choice was between Chelsea and Arsenal. I chose Arsenal because of the club's philosophy and stability. I adore Arsenal, Wenger really wanted me and I wasn't sure Di Matteo knows who I am."
On joining Arsenal instead of Chelsea.

"I can't help that I'm gorgeous."
In an anti-homophobia advert.

MESUT OZIL

"If you're not excited about watching Ozil you don't love football."
Arsene Wenger.

THE 2014 FA CUP FINAL

"We've had to dig deep into our archive because it's so long since they've won anything."
Adrian Chiles on ITV. Supporter of West Bromwich Albion, who had, at that point, gone 46 years "without a trophy".

"You almost want Arsenal to be put out of their misery."
Adrian Chiles again.

"Tomas (Rosicky) and me were physically sick watching."
Jack Wilshere, watching on the bench as Arsenal went 2-0 down.

"It was mind-blowing, I have dreamt about this day for many years as a young kid coming through and it hasn't quite sunk in yet."
Aaron Ramsey.

"You could tell that they were dropping off a bit but I felt that we were in control and we took advantage of that in the end.

"In the second half of extra time, at 2-2, things are going through your mind about penalties. It was important to try and keep going even though the legs didn't want to and I managed to get into the box and score the winner."
Ramsey again.

"We started every season with a handicap. Before the season even started the press were only talking about trophies. It started to get into everyone's heads.

We felt people were waiting for the chance to catch us out and we started the season under pressure, that explains the first match we lost (against Villa).

"(Wenger) deserves it because he believed in us, he gave each of us our chance. All those years he was criticised very much ... (at this point Bac broke down in tears) We sweated blood for quite a few years. I'm happy for him and all the club, because there are a lot of people behind the scenes."
Bacary Sagna.

"It was more important today than all the others. Twice we had won the double, so we had already won something and were not under the pressure we were under here.

"It is a feeling of relief and happiness as we were under severe pressure to win and we didn't start well of course. Hull started stronger and you could see we were hesitant. We demonstrated how to respond to being 2-0 down but we also demonstrated how not to start an FA Cup final.

"It is a big moment to win and when it happens after a long time it sometimes comes with suffering so it was a great moment."
Wenger.

"Boom. Trophy. Mind the gap."
Lee Dixon, having left the ITV studio and switched his phone on.

"Ja Gunners, Ja!"
Musut Ozil to a tv camera, a quote that quickly became his catchphrase.

THE 2015 FA CUP FINAL

"I felt physically sick."
Villa manager Tim Sherwood.

"I want to thank the manager for picking me and having faith in me and hopefully I repaid him. I missed all this last year. To be part of it this year is a dream come true. My family are here and I have worked so hard, as has everyone to do this. I also want to thank the physios and everyone who has looked after me. This is for them."
Theo Walcott.

"We have shown that we are a real team and can deal with pressure. I congratulate the players, the staff and the fans. We are so happy tonight. I had a difficult week to pick the team. But when confidence and sprit is so good it helps. Look, I am very proud. Our club is doing well and if I can personally do well then it's even better."
Arsene Wenger.

"Alexis Sanchez scores an outstanding goal, there's not much you can do about that one, but we were lucky not go behind earlier, we were holding on a bit. But to concede again from a set piece is gruelling. You almost don't mind if they open you up but to be honest you have to take your medicine at 3-0 and then to concede one at the death was a kick in the privates."
Sherwood again.

"We gave the fans nothing to cheer about today but I can promise them it will get better. We don't want to be scraping relegation next season."
Sherwood, a few months before he was sacked, with Villa rock bottom of the league and heading for relegation.

PART FIVE: MISCELLANEOUS
JOHN PEEL

"Frankly I listen to music with no concern whatever for the race, colour religion, preference in breakfast foods, height, shoe size or whatever you like of the music makers. The only footling prejudice I do permit myself is this: musicians I suspect supporting Everton or Arsenal have a bugger of a time getting their ponderous tripe on to the programme."
In response to accusations that he played too much black music - and too much white music.

BRIAN CLOUGH

"Nothing short of incredible. I'm loath to confess they could be as good as us. They are brilliant. It sticks in the craw a little bit because nobody likes Arsenal! Of course there's a Frenchman in charge, Wenger, and not many English people like Frenchmen (but) he is a top, top manager."
Clough after Arsenal beat Nottingham Forest's record of 42 games without defeat, by coming from 3-1 down to beat Middlesbrough 5-3, early in the 2004-05 season. Clough died of cancer less than a month after this match.

"I remember watching his teams play and I would say that the Forest side of the late 1970s will go down in history as one of the all-time greats. It is not an exaggeration to say that I was truly touched recently when he complimented the way this current Arsenal side plays and that we deserved to break his record."
Wenger, putting aside the remark about Frenchmen, in a tribute to Clough after his death.

RUUD VAN NISTLEROOY

"He tries it on in every match and somehow gets away with his butter-wouldn't-melt-in-his-mouth act. I think he actually spends as much time on the floor, rolling around, as he does scoring goals. I find it hard to respect someone like him."
Ashley Cole.

"He's always complaining, whingeing. To me he's deceitful as well as being a nasty piece of work ... He's a great player, I can't deny it ... but for me the man is a cheat and a thief (he) is a coward who is sneaky in the way he goes about fouling other players. Everyone thinks he's a nice guy but in fact he's a son of a bitch."
Patrick Vieira on a red card van Nistlerooy helped him earn at Old Trafford in 2003.

"There was a team aggression towards him. He took a dive, feigned injury and Vieira was sent off. We'd had enough of him and any respect went."
Martin Keown, explaining the motivation for leaping in RVN's face after he missed a last-minute penalty.

"You cannot tell me that Vieira is the devil and that Van Nistelrooy is an angel. Van Nistelrooy looks a nice boy, but on the pitch he doesn't always behave fairly. We saw Van Nistelrooy went for him. I think it is cheating."
Arsene Wenger.

"Arsenal may have worn yellow yesterday but they were tainted with red. The face of the beautiful game was ravaged with scars and tears. There is a thin line between celebrating and gloating and Arsenal trampled over it at Old Trafford with a shocking lack of class."
The Times Matt Dickinson, giving the lie to any suggestion of anti-Arsenal bias.

"A mewling bunch of juveniles that frequently masquerade as a team."
Martin Samuels, doing likewise.

GRAHAM POLL

"During United's 4-2 win at Arsenal in February 2005, Rooney infamously swore at me 27 times in the first half alone. Yet I considered my performance in that match to be the finest in all of my 329 Premier League games."
Poll in his column for the Mail.

"Successful man-management."
On his decision not to send Wayne Rooney off, after Rooney swore at him 27 times.

JOSE MOURINHO

"I know we live in a world where we have only winners and losers, but once a sport encourages teams who refuse to take the initiative, the sport is in danger."
Wenger on Mourinho's tactics.

"He is a specialist in failure."
On Arsene Wenger.

"I think he is one of these people who is a voyeur. He likes to watch other people. There are some guys who, when they are at home, they have a big telescope to see what happens in other families. He speaks and speaks and speaks about Chelsea."
Mourinho, before Chelsea's trip to Arsenal in 2005-06.

"He's out of order, disconnected with reality and disrespectful. When you give success to stupid people, it makes them more stupid sometimes and not more intelligent."
Wenger's reply.

"At Stamford Bridge, we have a file of quotes from Mr Wenger about Chelsea football club in the last 12 months - it is not a file of five pages. It is a file of 120 pages so we have a very strong reaction. My objective is that it is enough."
Mourinho, offering an insight into the workload of his black propaganda outfit.

"Unlike Arsenal, we sought success and tried to build it through a concept of the game using English players."
Mourinho in 2007.

"I don't see especially that Chelsea play more English players than we do. Who have they produced, homegrown? Just one, John Terry."
Wenger's reply.

"Instead of speaking about Real Madrid, Mr Wenger should speak about Arsenal and explain how he lost 2-0 against a team in the Champions League for the first time (Braga in 2010). The history about the young kids is getting old now. Sagna, Clichy, Walcott, Fabregas, Song, Nasri, Van Persie, Arshavin are not kids. They are all top players."
Mourinho's response after Wenger suggested Madrid had deliberately picked up two bookings in a Champions League game, to avoid getting suspensions in the knock-out stages.

DARA O'BRIAIN

"I'm sorry; it's a pleasure to watch them. Even if we're not there, it's still a rush to be thereabouts. I did my time in the early 90s when it was John Jensen and Eddie McGoldrick and we couldn't buy a goal. And you want me to tear my hair out now, when I've got Fabregas and Arshavin in front of me and Wilshere and Vela waiting in the wings?"

PIERS MORGAN
The majesty of the world's greatest professional wind-up merchant, via Twitter.

"Wenger trusts in Chamakh, Arshavin, Ramsey, Squillaci, Gervinho - why I no longer trust in him."

"What DOES Wenger see in Ramsey? A complete and utter liability"
Piers lets rip during a Champions League defeat to Olympiakos, December 2012.

"Last year I put sustained pressure on under-performing Wenger & Ramsey. Now we see the results. The words 'Thanks, Piers' wouldn't go amiss."

"Still slightly bemused by what I am supposed to be apologising to Wenger for - winning nothing for 8yrs or selling Van Pursestrings to Utd?"

"Dream finish? A 94th minute Van Pursestrings own goal to seal our win. #Afc #ChickensComingHomeToRoost"
Piers on Arsenal's trip to Old Trafford in November 2014.

"We're top of the league and about to annihilate United. We're back."
Piers before the trip to Old Trafford again. Arsenal lost 1-0.

"I've supported Arsenal for 44 years, and will until I die. Not sure what's so 'fickle' or 'plastic' about that."

A NOTE ON SOURCES & STRUCTURE
The idea for this book came while I was standing in a queue at Waterstones in Maidstone and saw a book entitled, "The Wit & Wisdom of Harry Redknapp" for sale in a pile by the counter. It was, as I suspected, a fairly slim volume, but I thought a heftier quote book dedicated to the Arsenal had a lot more potential.

I'd already read a substantial number of biographies and autobiographies while researching "Arsenal: The French Connection," but it became clear that I'd really only scratched the surface of the literature devoted to the club. Thanks to Greg Adams of GCR books I was able to get my hands on a number of books by pre-war Arsenal players, while Tony Attwood of the Arsenal Independent Supporters Association pointed me in the direction of a number of useful websites, not least his own www.blog.woolwicharsenal.co.uk/

These were invaluable in compiling the first section. Quotes became more fashionable in national newspapers after 1945, which made the later sections significantly easier to put together and by the time we reached the Arsene Wenger era the amount of source material had increased exponentially.

Where possible a source has been included for every quote, though in some cases, such as when the quote came from a press conference attended by multiple reporters, no attribution was possible. Some quotes have appeared on multiple websites without any indication where they originated from and in a few cases the quotes used came from press conferences I attended personally, from conversations I had with players, or from public events I attended.

The structure is loosely chronological, with some sections devoted to individuals and others dedicated to matches. Not every individual who deserves a section has one, nor does every "big" game.

In terms of style, the format owes a lot to the "Said and Done" Column by David Hills in the Observer, which has consistently used quotes to expose the idiocy and hypocrisy of footballers and chairmen.

BOOKS:

Arsenal: The French Connection by Fred Atkins (GCR Books, 2012)
John Spurling, "Rebels With A Cause" (Mainstream 2004).
Leslie Knighton, "Behind the Scenes in Big Football."Stanley Paul & Co, 1948.
Eddie Hapgood, "Football Ambassador," reprinted by GCR Books, 2009.
Herbert Chapman On Football, reprinted by GCR Books, 2010
Cliff Bastin Remembers, reprinted by GCR Books, 2010.
John Peel, Margrave of the Marshes: His Autobiography, Corgi, 2006.
Brian Glanville, "Wright or Wrong".
Bob Wilson, "My Autobiography," Hodder, 2004.
Charlie George, "My Story," Century, 2005.
"We All Live In A Perry Groves World," by Perry Groves and John McShane, John Blake 2006.
"The Glory and the Grief," by George Graham, Andre Deutsch, 1996.
"How Not To Be A Professional Footballer," by Paul Merson, Harper Sport, 2012.
"Addicted," by Tony Adams, Willow, 1999.
"Mr Wright, The Explosive Autobiography of Ian Wright," by Ian Wright, Willow, 1997.
"Fever Pitch," by Nick Hornby, Penguin, 2012.
"Vieira, My Autobigraphy," by Patrick Vieira, Orion, 2006.
Theo Walcott, "Growing Up Fast," Corgi, 2012.
"Stillness and Speed: My Story," by Dennis Bergkamp, Simon & Schuster, 2014.
"Safe Hands," by David Seaman, Orion, 2000.
"Wenger, The Making of a Legend," by Jasper Rees, Short Books, 2003.
"Arsene Wenger: The Biography," by Xavier Rivoire, Autrum, 2008.
"A Fleur de Peau," by Emmanuel Petit, Prolongations, 2008.
"My Defence," Ashley Cole, Headline, 2006.
"Anelka, par Nicholas Anelka," by Arnuad Ramsay, Hugo & Cie, 2012.
"Footballeur," by Robert Pires, Yellow Jersey, 2004.
"Red," by Gary Neville, Corgi, 2012.
Sol Campbell - The Authorised Biography, by Simon Astaire, Spellbinding Media, 2014.
"La parole est a la defense," by William Gallas, Moment, 2012.

WEBSITES:

www.thearsenalcollective.com
http://www.blog.woolwicharsenal.co.uk/
theclockend.com
Daily Post
www.iamplayr.com
www.arsenalinsider.com
Sportlobster TV.
weateallthepies.com
arseblog.com

Daily Telegraph
www.bbc.co.uk
www.guardian.co.uk
www.sport.co.uk
www.thebackheel.wordpress.com
www.wrightanddavis.co.uk is a website run by Sally Davis and an extensive record of Henry Norris's day-to-day activities
www.arsenal-mania.com
www.thearsenalcollective.com
www.espn.com
www.liverpoolfc.com
www.mightyleeds.co.uk
www.7amkickoff
www.442.com
www.LFChistory.net
www.arshavin.eu
arsenal.com
twitter.com

MAGAZINES

Shoot!
When Saturday Comes

NEWSPAPERS

The Times Archive
The Guardian
The Daily Mail
The Daily Mirror
The Kentish Gazette
The Islington Gazette
Daily Herald
The Sunday Times
The Ipswich Star
The Independent
The Observer
The Evening Standard
The Sun
Shoot!
L'Equipe
France Football
The News of the World

FILM

The Arsenal Stadium Mystery

ENDQUOTE

"I have periods where I am tired, yes. It's true that the close season makes people think you're resting but it's during that that you work the most. I got in the habit of working all the time. I think I must have been lazy in a previous life and was punished to come back in a very tiring and stressful job.

"I'd like to go to Tahiti for a month but I can't. From time to time I would like to because I'm running out of time. Everyone gets older. When I arrive at the gates of Heaven the Good Lord will ask 'what did you do in your life?' I will respond 'I tried to win football matches.' He will say: 'Are you certain that's all?' But, well, that's the story of my life."

Arsene Wenger in 2011, to the French radio station RTL.

ABOUT THE COMPILER

Fred Atkins was born in Maidstone in 1973 and spent much of his formative years at Maidstone United's Athletic Ground. He attended Oakwood Park Grammar School, Sussex University and the Institut d'Etudes Politiques in Strasbourg.

After graduation he drifted into the arena of unemployment and barely noticed a difference. He then spent three years as an English teacher, in his words "teaching foreign students how to swear", before stumbling into journalism with the Maidstone News.

He became sports editor of the Kent Messenger and went on to work for the Associated Press, covering the England cricket team for five years, including two Ashes series and the 2009 Twenty20 World Cup. He now works as a copy writer and as the media manager and website editor for the Lashings All-Stars cricket team.

Fred is the author of three books. "The Double, the story of Maidstone United's 2001-2002 season", followed by "Tour de Kent" (published by Breedon Books in 2009) and "Arsenal: The French Connection" (published by GCR Books in 2012).

Fred also edited "Stuck In A Moment" by Stewart Taylor, which was longlisted for the 2014 William Hill Award.

His first novel, "Welcome to Kent" will be published during the 2016-17 season.

He lives in Allington with his wife Wendy and daughter, Sylvia.

Arsenal: The French Connection was first published in 2012 and is now available for the first time as a paperback and on Kindle.

FOUR FOUR TWO MAGAZINE gave it four stars out of five and called it:
'a detailed trawl through Wenger's career is laced with humour drier than a bottle of Cabernet Sauvignon, revealing a fine appreciation of both the game and our relationship with our cross channel freres.'

The "When Saturday Comes" reviewer was upset by the "Puerile jibes about Alex Ferguson."
Can there be any higher recommendation?

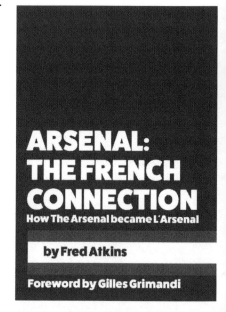

Maidstone Express

Just £2.99! *(Where sold)*

The first novel by Fred Atkins - available soon on www.amazon.co.uk

Officially the UK's SHITTEST newspaper

Welcome to Kent ...

... sorry about the racists

by Fred Atkins

1st with the SCOOPS!

DJ chief suspect as girl vanishes

PETER Pope, host of the Downs FM morning show, was in police custody last night, after a Maidstone schoolgirl disappeared during a trip to Hythe Zoo
... Page 3

Trio sought after 'dog shit' attack

Maidstone Police were hunting for three teens last night after Council Leader Katrina Kitchener was allegedly assaulted with a "bag of dog shit"
... Page 5

Calls to 'brick up' Channel Tunnel

MEDIA mogul Gert Smuts last night urged the UK government to build a wall at the entrance to the Channel Tunnel
... Page 3

Mob target Dr Paedo's house

The Bower Mount Road house of the "Barming Flasher" was burnt to the ground last night after a mob reacted angrily to a 'lenient' sentence
... Page 9

Manager 'wants to win' match

A LOCAL football manager has told assorted reporters that he wants to "win" Saturday's match. And failing that draw it.
... Page 54

The Maidstone Express is officially 'Britain's Shittest Paper' for the fourth consecutive year, according to a Guardian survey.

It churns out stories about killer pot holes, custard powder shortages and newsagents that sell out of date pasties.

The editor is suicidal, the chief reporter is a racist and there's a sex offender running the sports desk.

Libel

When they accidentally libel a local surgeon the Express is on the brink of collapse, until it's rescued by a billionaire buy-to-let tycoon from South Africa.

He installs two talented but suspect executives and a "technology consultant" and bankrolls a circulation war with the Express's reputable rival, the Maidstone Herald.

The Herald's Star reporter Mo Godwin once dreamed getting a job at the Daily Mail and coming up with a story so ludicrous it would shut the paper down.

Now he's trying to track down a girl who vanished into thin air during a school trip, with local radio DJ Peter Pope the chief suspect.

Godwin is convinced his former employers at the Express are hacking his stories but his bosses think he's making excuses.

When the local priest's adopted daughter is abducted and no one seems interested in finding her he has the chance to solve both cases, save his newspaper and his career – all while trying to stop his best friend from marrying a piece of American trailer trash twice his age.

Welcome to Kent is an allegory of the hacking scandal, a satire of smal-town racism and a coruscating account of life on a provincial newspaper.

Available soon as an e-book on Amazon.

KENT: Lovely. But slightly racist.

Printed in Great Britain
by Amazon